To Train Up A Child

by

Michael & Debi Pearl

No Greater Joy Ministries, Inc.
1000 Pearl Road
Pleasantville, TN 37147
United States of America
www.NoGreaterJoy.org

Introduction

This book is not about discipline, nor problem children. The emphasis is on the training of a child before the need to discipline arises. It is apparent that, though they expect obedience, most parents never attempt to train their child to obey. They wait until his behavior becomes unbearable and then explode. With proper training, discipline can be reduced to 5% of what many now practice. As you come to understand the difference between training and discipline, you will have a renewed vision for your family—no more raised voices, no contention, no bad attitudes, fewer spankings, a cheerful atmosphere in the home, and total obedience from your children.

Any parent with an emotional maturity level higher than the average thirteen-year-old can, with a proper vision and knowledge of the technique, have happy obedient children. This is not a theory; it is a practical reality that has been successfully applied many times over.

One couple we know was stressed out with the conflict of their three young children. After spending the weekend with us and hearing some of these principles, they changed their tactics. One week later, they exclaimed, "I can't believe it; we went to a friend's house, and when I told my children to do something, they immediately, without question, obeyed."

These truths are not new, deep insights from the professional world of research, but rather, the same principles the Amish use to train their stubborn mules, the same technique God uses to train His children. These principles are profoundly simple and extremely obvious. After examining them with us, you will say, "I knew that all along. Where have I been? It's so obvious."

This book could not have been possible without the many friends who recklessly and, at the time, unknowingly contributed to the many examples found in these pages. Little did they know that their parenting was being scrutinized and documented.

To all the children named Johnny, I apologize. Some name had to be used to keep all others anonymous.

Although the majority of the text bears the name of Michael, and the smaller portion that of Debi, she played a constant role as critic and editor. Many of the creative ideas are hers. Without her I could neither have been successful as a parent, nor have written this little book on the subject.

Update

Our children are now grown. Rebekah is happily married and has given us our first grandchild. Nathan is happily married and Gabriel owns his own home. The two girls, Shalom and Shoshanna, are now 18 and 20 as of this printing. They are a great help to us in the ministry.

This is the fourteenth printing of this book. We continue to fill orders for thousands of books every month. We trust that this book will be a blessing to you and to your family as you train up your children.

Michael & Debi Pearl

Table of Contents

To Train Up a Child 1
Childish Nature 14
Parental Anger 22
Tying Strings 26
The Rod 35
Applying the Rod 46
Philosophy of the Rod 50
Selective Subjection 52
Training Examples 56
Safety Training 66
Potty Untraining 70
Child Labor 74
Attitude Training 77
Emotional Control 84
Training in Self-Indulgence 88
Bullies 90
Religious Whips 92
Imitations 94
Homeschool Makes No Fools 96
Personal 98
Conclusion 107

CHAPTER 1

To Train Up a Child

SWITCH YOUR KIDS

When you tell some parents they need to switch their children, they respond, "I would if I could find someone willing to trade." I have had children in my house that were enough to give an electric wheat grinder a nervous breakdown. Their parents looked like escapees from a WWII Polish boxcar. Another hour with those kids and I would have been searching the yellow pages for discount vasectomies. While we tried to sit and talk, the children were constantly running in and out of doors, complaining of ill treatment from the others, begging to go or stay or eat, or demanding a toy that another child would not relinquish. The mother had to continually jump up and rescue some breakable object. She said, "No," six hundred sixty-six times in the space of two hours. She spanked each child two or three times—usually with her hand on top of a diaper. Other than misaligning the child's spine, it seemed to have had no effect.

When we speak of consistently rewarding every transgression with a switching (not a karate chop to the lower backbone), some mothers can only see themselves further brutalizing children for whom it will do no good. Their discipline is just "laying down a field of fire" to give themselves sufficient cover to get through to the next task. They have no hope of conquering the child's will. They just desire to create enough diversion to accomplish their own mission.

Another mother walked into my house with her little ones and sat down to talk. She said to them, "Go out in the sunroom and play, and don't bother Mama unless you need something." For the next two hours we were not even aware the children were present—except when a little one came in holding herself saying, "Pee-pee, Mama." They played together well, resolved their own conflicts, and didn't expect attention when one of the girls turned the rocking horse over and got a knot on her head. They didn't run in and out—they were told not to.

This mother did not spank her children while at my house, and she did not need to rebuke them. She looked rested. When she called the children to go home, one asked, "Mama, can I stay and play with Shoshanna?" Mother answered, "No, not today. We have work to do at home." As he lifted his arms, his mother picked him up. Hugging his mother's neck, he said, "I love you, Mama."

This young mother said to me, "My children want to please me. They try so hard to do everything I say. We have such fun together." She is looking forward to having more children. They are the joy of her life.

By the grace of God and through the simple, Biblical principles found in these pages, with determination and an open heart, this mother has trained up children that bring her joy and honor.

OBEDIENCE TRAINING

Training does not necessarily require that the trainee be capable of reason; even mice and rats can be trained to respond to stimuli. Careful training can make a dog perfectly obedient. If a seeing-eye dog can be trained to reliably lead a blind man through the obstacles of a city street, shouldn't a parent expect more out of an intelligent child? A dog can be trained not to touch a tasty morsel laid in front of him. Can't a child be trained not to touch? A dog can be trained to come, stay, sit, be quiet, or fetch upon command. You may not have trained your dog that well, yet every day someone accomplishes it on the dumbest of mutts. Even a clumsy teenager can be trained to be an effective trainer in a dog obedience school.

If you wait until your dog is displaying unacceptable behavior before you rebuke (or kick) him, you will have a foot-shy mutt that is always sulking around to see what he can get away with before being screamed at. Where there is an absence of training, you can no more rebuke and whip a child into acceptable behavior than you can the family dog. No amount of discipline can make up for a lack of training.

Proper training always works with every child. To neglect training is to create miserable circumstances for you and your child. Out of ignorance many have bypassed training and expected discipline alone to effect proper behavior. It hasn't worked.

"TENNN—HUTT!!"

When headstrong young men join the military, the first thing they are taught is to stand still. The many hours of close-order-drill are to teach and reinforce submission of the will. "Attention!" pronounced,

"TENNN—HUTT!!" is the beginning of all maneuvers. Just think of the relief that it would bring if by one command you could gain the absolute, concentrated attention of all your children. A sergeant can call his men to attention and then ignore them, without explanation, and they will continue to stand frozen in that position until they fall out unconscious. The maneuvers "Right flank, Left flank, Companeeey—Halt" have no value in war except that they condition the men to instant, unquestioning obedience.

As in the military, all maneuvers in the home begin with a call to attention. Three-fourths of all home discipline problems would be solved if you could instantly gain your child's silence and unmoving attention. "TO THE REAR—MARCH" translated into family language would be: "Leave the room," or, "Go to bed." Without question they would turn and go. This is normal in the well-trained family.

"WHOA, HORSE"

We live in a horse and buggy community where someone is always training a new horse. When you get into a buggy to go down a narrow, winding, state highway filled with eighteen-wheelers and logging trucks, you must have a totally submissive horse. You cannot depend on whipping him into submission. One mistake and the young men will again be making several new pine boxes and digging six-foot deep holes in the orchard.

A horse is first trained to stand still and submit to being caught and handled. He must not fear the bridle or harness. He must stand still while thirteen children step in front of the iron wheels to climb into the buggy. When stopped at the end of a driveway, waiting for the traffic to clear, he must not exercise his will to step out in front of eighty thousand pounds of speeding truck.

Horse training involves preparing the horse to respond correctly in all future situations to which he will be exposed. This training is done in a controlled environment where circumstances are created to test and condition the horse's responses. This is done by taking him through various paces. To train him to stop, as you hold the bridle and lead the horse, you say, "Whoa," and then stop. Since you have a tight hold on the bridle, he must stop. After just a few times, the horse will stop at just your command.

The trainer establishes the tone of voice at which the horse is to respond. If you speak in a normal tone the horse will obey. If you scream "Whoa!!" then in the future the horse will not stop unless the command is screamed the same way. One such farmer trained his horses with a wild, frantic bellow. Most of his neighbors, who speak quietly to their horses, find it difficult to control his horses because of their inability to raise their voices in vehemence.

SPEAK TO ME ONLY

I was logging with a fifteen-hundred-pound mule that sometimes wanted to run away with the log. In moments of stress (actually I was panic stricken), I found myself frantically YELLING commands. The owner would patiently caution me, "Speak quietly and calmly or he will pay no attention." I never did learn the art of calmly saying, "Whoa" to a runaway mule pulling a twenty-five foot, white oak log with my foot hung in the trace chain. The point to remember is that animals learn to identify not only the sound but also the tone.

If you raise your voice when giving a command to your child, he will learn to associate your tone and sound level with your intention. If you have trained him to respond to a bellow, don't blame him if he ignores your first thirteen "suggestions" while waiting for your fevered pitch to reach the point where he interprets it to be a real command.

TRAINING, NOT DISCIPLINE

"Train up a child in the way he should go: and when he is old, he will not depart from it (Prov. 22:6)." Train up—not beat up. Train up—not discipline up. Train up—not educate up. Train up—not "positive affirmation" up. Training is the most often missed element in child rearing. A child needs more than "obedience training," but without it discipline is insufficient.

Parents should not wait until their child's behavior becomes unacceptable before they commence training—which would be discipline. Training is not discipline. Discipline is a part of training but is insufficient in itself to effect proper behavior. Training is the conditioning of the child's mind before the crisis arises. It is preparation for future, instant, unquestioning obedience. An athlete trains before he competes. Animals, including wild ones, are conditioned to respond to the trainer's voice command.

The frustration parents experience results from their failure to train. Their problem is not "bad" children, just bad training. The "strong willed," the hyperactive, the highly intelligent, and the easily bored all need training, and training is effective on all.

Understand, at this point we are not talking about producing godly children, just happy and obedient children. The principles for training young children to instantly obey can be applied by non-Christians as well as Christians. As children get older, the character and teaching of the trainer plays a more significant role.

TRAINING NOT TO TOUCH

There is a lot of satisfaction to be gained in training up a child. It is easy, yet challenging. When my children were able to crawl (in the case of one, roll) around the room, I set up training sessions.

Try it yourself. Place an appealing object where they can reach it, maybe in a "No-No" corner or on the apple juice table (another name for the coffee table). When they spy it and make a dive for it, in a calm voice say, "No, don't touch that." Since they are already familiar with the word "No," they will pause, look at you in wonder and then turn around and grab it. Switch their hand once and simultaneously say, "No." Remember, you are not disciplining, you are training. One spat with a little switch is enough. They will again pull back their hand and consider the relationship between the object, their desire, the command, and the little reinforcing pain. It may take several times, but if you are consistent, they will learn to consistently obey, even in your absence.

PLANT YOUR TREE IN THE MIDST OF THE GARDEN

When God wanted to "train" his first two children not to touch, He did not place the forbidden object out of their reach. Instead, He placed the *"tree of knowledge of good and evil"* in the *"midst of the garden (Gen.3:3)."* Since it was in the middle of the garden, they would be exposed to its temptation more often. God's purpose was not to save the tree, but rather, to train the couple.

Note the name of the tree was not just "knowledge of evil," but, *"knowledge of good and evil."* By exercising their wills not to eat, they would have learned the meaning of *"good"* as well as *"evil."* Eating the tree was not the only way in which they could come to knowledge of good and evil, but it was a forbidden shortcut.

By placing a forbidden object within reach of the children, and then enforcing your command to not touch it, every time the children pass the 'No-No' object (their "tree of knowledge of good and evil"), they are gaining knowledge of **good and evil** from the standpoint of an overcomer. As with Adam and Eve in the garden, the object and the touching of it is, in itself, of no consequence; but the attachment of a command to it makes it a moral "factory" where character is produced. By your enforcement, your children are learning about moral government, duty, responsibility, and, in the event of failure, accountability, rewards, and punishment. In the here and now, they are also learning not to touch, which makes a child's social life a lot more pleasant.

It just takes a few minutes to train a child not to touch a given object. Most children can be brought into complete and joyous subjection in just three days. Thereafter, if you continue to be faithful, the children will remain happy and obedient. By obedient, I mean you will never need to tell them twice. If you expect to receive instant obedience, and you train them to that end, you will be successful. It will take extra time to train, but once the children are in general subjection, the time saved will be extraordinary. Some people say, "Child-proof your home." I say, "Home-proof your child."

TOUCHY SITUATIONS
Have you ever been the victim of tiny, inquisitive hands? A very young child, not yet walking, is keen on wanting to grab any object of interest. There is no fault in this, but sometimes it can be annoying. When you are holding a baby and he keeps pulling off your glasses, you cannot explain to him the impropriety of such socially crude behavior. The little tot is not yet moved by fear of rejection. So, do you try to restrain him where he can't get to your face? No, you train him not to touch. Once you train an infant to respond to the command "No," then you will have control in every area where you can give a command.

Set up training situations. For example, using your glasses as bait, place the child where he can easily reach them. Look him squarely in the eye. When he reaches out to grab them, don't pull back; don't defend yourself. Calmly say, "No." If anything, lower your voice; don't raise it. Don't sound more serious than usual. Remember you are establishing a vocal pattern to be used the rest of his youth. If he reaches out to touch your glasses, again say, "No," and accompany your command with minor pain. He will pull his hand back and try to comprehend the association of grabbing the glasses with the pain. (I usually just thumped their little hand with my index finger. I have never known a child to cry from this. They don't even know that I did it. They think that it was the glasses, or perhaps the "No" itself that caused their pain.) Inevitably, he will return to the bait to test his new theory. Sure enough, the glasses again cause pain and the pain is accompanied with a quiet, little "No." It may take one or two more tries for him to give up his career as glasses snatcher, but he will.

Through this process, the child will associate the pain with the word "No." There comes a time when your word alone is sufficient to gain obedience.

Through this kind of early training you can stop him from assaulting his mother with a bottle held by the nipple. The same holds true for hair and beard pulling. You name it; the infant can be trained to obey. Do you want to wrestle with him through his entire youth, nagging him into compliance, threatening, placing things out of reach, fearing what he might get into next? Wouldn't it be better to take a little time to train him? If nothing else, training will result in saving you time.

I know a mother who must call a baby-sitter every time she takes a shower. You should be able to take a nap and expect to find the house in order when you awake.

OBEDIENCE TRAINING—*BITING BABIES*

One particularly painful experience of nursing mothers is the biting baby. My wife did not waste time finding a cure. When the baby bit, she pulled hair (an alternative has to be sought for bald-headed babies). Understand, the baby is not being punished, just conditioned. A baby learns not to stick his finger in his eyes or bite his tongue through the negative associations accompanying it. It requires no understanding or reasoning. Somewhere in the brain, that information is unconsciously stored. After biting two or three times, and experiencing pain in association with each bite, the child programs that information away for his own comfort. The biting habit is cured before it starts. This is not discipline. It is obedience training.

OBEDIENCE TRAINING—*BOWLS AND BABIES*

The mother clumsily holds her cereal bowl at arm's length as she wrestles her infant for supremacy. When she places the bowl out of the baby's reach, he is taught that it is off limits only if it is out of reach. To train him, place the bowl within easy reach. When he reaches for it, say, "No," and thump his hand. He will pull his hand back, momentarily look alarmed, and then reach again. Repeat the action of saying, "No" in a calm voice, and thump his hand. After several times, you will be able to eat in peace.

After several occasions of responding to a thump and the word "No," the voice command alone soon becomes sufficient to direct the child's behavior. Again, keep in mind, the baby is not being punished, just conditioned. The thump is not a substitute rod. It is reinforcement to obedience training.

COME WHEN I CALL YOU

One father tells of his training sessions with each new toddler. He sets aside an evening for "booty" camp, which is a boot camp for toddlers. The child of ten to twelve months is left alone to become deeply interested in a toy or some delightful object. From across the room or just inside another room, the father calls the child. If the child ignores the call, the father goes to him and explains the necessity of immediately coming when called, and then leads him through the steps of obedience by walking him over to the place from which he was called.

He is returned to the toy and left alone long enough to again become engrossed. The father calls again. If the child ignores the call, the father gives additional explanation and a repeat of the practiced walk. The parent, having assured himself that the child understands what is expected of him, goes back to call again. This time if the child does not respond immediately, the father administers one or two swats with a switch and then continues the exercise until the child readily responds to his summons. Thereafter, until the child leaves home, the parent can expect the child to drop everything and come when called. As long as parents remain consistent, the child will consistently obey. This "obedience training" is conducted with quiet patience. The spanking is not punishment. It is to give weight to your words.

NEVER TOO YOUNG TO TRAIN

A newborn soon needs training. Parents that put off training until their child is old enough to discuss issues or receive explanations will find he has become a terror long before he understands the meaning of the word.

As a mother attempts to lower her child into the crib, he stiffens, takes a deep breath, and bellows. The battle for control has begun in earnest. Someone is going to be conditioned. Either the tenderhearted mother will cave in to the child's self-centered demands (training the child to get his way by crying) or he will be allowed to cry (thus learning that crying is counterproductive). Crying because of genuine physical need is the infant's only voice to the outside world, but crying in order to manipulate others into constant servitude should never be rewarded. Otherwise, you will reinforce the child's growing self-centeredness, which will eventually become socially intolerable.

STEPS TO OBEDIENCE

One of our girls, who developed mobility early, had a fascination with crawling up stairs. At five months she was too unknowing to be punished for disobedience. But for her own good we attempted to train her not to climb the stairs by coordinating the voice command of "No" with little spats on her bare legs. The switch was a twelve-inch long, one-eighth-inch diameter sprig from a willow tree.

Such was her fascination with climbing, that she continued to climb, ignoring the spankings. Spanking is supposed to work, but it seemed that at her young age her little brain couldn't maintain the association. So I laid the switch on the bottom step. We later observed her crawl to the stairs and start the ascent, only to halt at the first step and stare at the switch. She backed off and never again attempted to climb the stairs, even after the switch was removed.

EXCESSIVE DISCIPLINE

Disciplinary actions can become excessive and oppressive if you set aside the tool of training and depend on discipline alone to do the training. I observed a proud, stern father, ruling his children with a firm hand, and making sure everyone knew it. His rod was swift to fall, especially in the presence of company. His children trembled in his presence, fearing to incur his displeasure. I wondered why, if he was so firm and faithful to gain obedience, he had not achieved it before entering the public arena. I was impressed, but not in the way he hoped.

Except where the very smallest children are concerned, training at home almost entirely eliminates the need for public discipline. Yet, should the need arise in public, be discreet with your discipline and then go home and train so that you will not be placed in that difficult situation again.

TRAINING THE ORNERY AMISH BOY

As I sat talking with a local Amish fellow, a typical child training session developed. The twelve-month-old boy, sitting on his father's lap, suddenly developed a compulsion to slide to the floor. Due to the cold floor, the father directed the child to stay in his lap. The child stiffened and threw his arms up to lessen the father's grip and facilitate his slide to the floor. The father spoke to him in the German language (which I did not understand) and firmly placed him back in the sitting position. The child made dissenting noises and continued his attempt to dismount his father's lap. The father then spanked the child and spoke what I assumed to be reproving words. Seeing his mother across the room, the child began to cry and reach for her. This was understandable in any language. It was obvious that the child felt there would be more liberty with his mother.

At this point, I became highly interested in the proceedings. The child was attempting to go around the chain of command. Most fathers would have been glad to pass the troublesome child to his mother. If the child had been permitted to initiate the transfer, he would have been the one doing the training, not the parents. Mothers often run to their children in this situation, because they crave the gratification of being needed. But this mother was more concerned for her child's training than for her own sentiment. She appeared not to hear the child's plea.

The father then turned the child to face away from his mother. The determined fellow immediately understood that the battle lines had been drawn. He expressed his will to dominate by throwing his leg back over to the other side to face his mother. The father spanked the leg the child turned toward his mother and again spoke to him.

Now the battle was in full array. Someone was going to submit his will to the other. Either the father would confirm that this one-year-old could rule his parents, or the parents would confirm their authority. Everyone's happiness was at stake—as well as the soul of the child. The father was wise enough to know this was a test of authority. This episode had crossed over from "obedience training" to "discipline for attitude."

During the following forty-five minutes, the child shifted his legs fifteen times, and received a spanking each time. The father was as calm as a lazy porch swing on a Sunday afternoon. There was no hastiness or anger in his response. He did not take the disobedience personally. He had trained many horses and mules and knew the value of patient perseverance. In the end, the twelve-month-old submitted his will to his father, sat as he was placed, and became content—even cheerful.

Some will say, "But I couldn't take it emotionally." Sometimes it is difficult and trying to set aside your feelings for the sake of child training. It does involve emotional sacrifice. Yet, what is love but giving? When we know it will work to the temporal and eternal good of the child, it is a joy instead of a sacrifice.

If you know yourself to be angry or impatient, you may be carrying guilt that prevents you from being aggressive in disciplining your child. You may fear that your discipline is an act of your ego to dominate. You must deal with your own impurities for the sake of the child, for if he doesn't receive consistent and forceful training, he will greatly suffer.

BE ASSURED OF TWO THINGS

First, almost every small child will have at least one time in his young life when he will rebel against authority and take hold of the reins. This stubbornness is profound—amazing—a wonder that one so young could be so dedicated and persevering in rebellion. It is the kind of determination you would expect to find in a hardened revolutionary facing enemy indoctrination classes. Parents that are trained to expect it, and are prepared to persevere, will nonetheless stand in awe at the strength of the small child's will.

Second, if you are consistent in training, this attempt at total dominance will come only once in a child's life. If you win the confrontation, the child wins at the game of character development. If you weaken and allow the child to dominate, the child loses everything but his will to dominate. You must persevere for the sake of the child.

The cat that is prevented from coming into the house most of the time, but occasionally breaks through the barrier, will take the occasional success as impetus to always try to get in. However, if he is consistently kept out (100% of the time), he will lose the will to come in, even when the door is left open. You may kick him, slam the door on his tail, and throw him sixty feet, but if you occasionally allow him to stay in long enough to eat scraps off the floor or sleep on the couch, he will forever take the risk of running the gauntlet to get in. Your abuse may make him sufficiently wary to obey while you remain on guard, but he will still bolt through the door when he sees the opportunity.

On the other hand, dogs can be trained either to come in or stay out on command. The key again is consistency. If the dog learns through conditioning (consistent behavior on the part of the trainer) that he will never be allowed to violate his master's command, he will always obey. If parents carefully and consistently train up their children, their performance will be superior to that of a well-trained, seeing-eye dog.

NEGATIVE TRAINING

How many times have you observed children in the grocery store arena? A devious little kid sits up in the command seat of the shopping cart exercising his "childhood rights" to unlimited self-indulgence. The parent, fearfully but hopelessly, steers around the tempting "trees of knowledge of good and evil." Too late! The child spies the object of his unbridled lust. The battle is on. The child will either get what he wants or make his parent miserable. Either way, he conquers.

PURCHASED COMPLIANCE

One father proudly told of how he fearlessly overcame by promising the child ice cream if he would only wait until they left the store. Such compromises will only affirm the child in his commitment to terrorist tactics. You are not gaining control of the child; he is gaining control of you. All children are trained, some carelessly or negligently, and some, with varied degrees of forethought. All parental responses are conditioning the child's behavior, and are, therefore, training.

Parents who purchase compliance through promise of reward are turning their child into a racketeer, paid for protection. The child becomes the Mafia or union boss, and you take the role of intimidated businessman. If you are bargaining with a terrorist for one more day's reprieve from anguish, may you then strike a favorable deal, but if you are training up a child, you need to reconsider your methods. Allowing yourself to be intimidated into compromise will turn your child into a psychological bully.

DID YOU HEAR WHAT I SAID?

I observed a father tell his small boy not to touch a particular object. Having been trained to ignore mild commands, the child picked it up anyway. With irritation in his voice, the father demanded, "Give it to me." The child pretended not to hear. With anger, "Did you hear me? (Of course he did.) Hand it to Daddy." With mounting anger, "Johnnnieee, give it to Daddy, NOW!!" Finally, another decibel higher—hasty—angry—threatening, "JOHNNY!! Am I going to have to SPANK YOU?" By this time the father was aware of his embarrassing tone. He calmed his voice, and in an attempt to bring it to a conclusion, he leaned way out and extended his hand, making it easier for Johnny to comply. Because of his father's angry voice and burning eyes, Johnny assumed the temporary posture of, "Oh well, there will be another day."

But, instead of handing the object to the humbled, groping father, he held it in his general direction but down close to his body, forcing the father to advance even farther to retrieve it. The father, looking like a poor peasant receiving alms from some condescending royalty, submitted to the child's humiliation and reached to retrieve the object. And then, in a display of weakness, the father placed it out of the child's reach.

What did Johnny learn from this episode? He had his conviction reinforced that it is never necessary to obey a command the first, second, third, or even fourth time. No one expects him to. He has learned that it is permissible to grab anything within reach and to continue possessing it until the heat gets too great. He has learned not to respect authority, just strength (the day will come when he will be the stronger one). By the father's example, he has learned how to use anger. By the father's advance to take the object from his hand, he has learned how to "get in the last shot" and maintain his defiance. That father was effectively training his small child to be a rebel.

What has the father learned? He has learned that little Johnny is just a "strong-willed" child; that children go through unpleasant stages; that it is sometimes a very miserable and embarrassing thing to be a parent; that one has to watch a kid every minute and put things out of his reach; that the only things kids understand are force and anger. All of which are false. The father is reaping the harvest of his failure to train.

CHAPTER 2
Childish Nature

(Understanding a child's natural development)

"BEHOLD, THE SECOND WOE"!

Just last night while sitting in a meeting, I looked over to see a young mother struggling with her small child. He seemed determined to make her life as miserable as possible—and to destroy her reputation in the process. She had the "Why me?" look on her tired face. He kept defiantly throwing his bottle on the floor (assisted by her picking it up and handing it back to him) and making angry noises that forced the preacher to speak louder and louder. By increasing his embarrassing displays, the child forced her to put him down on the floor. He then proceeded to act as a circus clown, drawing attention away from the preacher. Finally he insisted on procuring a neighbor's property. When the frazzled mother tried to prevent his thievery and rescue the stolen goods, he kicked his legs like an eggbeater while screaming in protest.

It was enough to make you believe the Devil started out as an infant. I am just thankful that one-year-olds don't weigh two hundred pounds, or a lot more mothers would be victims of infant homicide. It causes one to understand where the concept of a "sinful nature" originated.

The mother knew that the child shouldn't be acting like this, but due to the child's limited intellectual development, she felt helpless. Older children and adults have their actions constrained by many mental and social factors. This child was not affected by peer-pressure, threat of embarrassment, or rejection. His life was one of unlimited, unrestrained self-indulgence. The parents were waiting for the child's understanding to develop so they could correct "bad" behavior. They helplessly watched while selfishness and meanness of spirit took root in a void of understanding.

What is the driving force in this child, and how can it be conquered? We need to understand some things about the nature of a child in order to institute appropriate training.

GOD-GIVEN SELF-CENTEREDNESS

For the purpose of moral development, God created us to exist in a constant state of need and dependence. These innate needs are most apparent in the small child. He needs food, warmth, companionship, entertainment, and a dry diaper. God has endowed him with strong, involuntary compulsions to taste, smell, hear, see, and a desire to touch and feel.

The desires and passions in the infant are not yet complete. As he matures, he will find himself possessed of ever-increasing, natural desires for things *"pleasant to the eyes,"* things *"good for food"* and for those things that will *"make one wise."* His growing humanity will give way to a desire to build, to know, to be appreciated, to be recognized, to succeed, to be a lover, and to survive in a secure state.

As infants grow, they learn to manipulate their surroundings to their own gratification. A smile, grunt, kicking of the feet, rolling and shaking the head, crying, and screaming all say, "Pick me up, feed me, look at me. Doesn't anyone realize I have urgent needs? What could be more important than *me*?"

An infant's world is no bigger than his needs. It is the only reality he knows. He soon learns that not only his needs but his "wants" can be readily satisfied as well. The infant cannot think in terms of duty, responsibility, or moral choice. He has no pride or humility—only desire. He comes, he sees, he takes. He is created that way. By nature, he is incapable of considering the needs of others. The child doesn't know you are tired and also in need of comfort.

The self-centeredness of infants and small children has all the appearances of a vice. But they are acting on natural, God-given impulses to meet their natural needs. They *"go astray as soon as they be born, speaking lies (Psalm 58:3)."* Yet, God does not impute the lie to them as sin. God reckons them as if they had no moral character, and therefore no responsibility. They do not possess the intellectual and moral maturity to say "No" to appetites. They cannot yet be held responsible. They begin life in innocent self-centeredness.

TO BLAME OR NOT TO BLAME

As the child gets older, say from eight to twelve months, the adults in his life begin to pay less attention to his demands, and a weaning process begins. The child is made to wait, told "No," and given boundaries. He must learn that he cannot always be first. If early training has not subdued the manifestations of his "selfishness," people begin to refer to him as "spoiled."

Guilty, frustrated parents are manipulated by the child's whining and crying. The spatting begins. The kid gets jerked around. Resentment builds. Adults begin to blame him, even compete with him.

The child feels this tension but doesn't lessen his demands. He connives, calculates, and resorts to angry tantrums. I have seen a two-year-old take a weapon and angrily strike his mother. The young child has not matured to a point where he can understand responsibility, weigh values, and make conscious decisions based on moral or social worth, but he certainly can mimic the criminal mind.

TOWARD UNDERSTANDING

What is happening? A short time ago the adults around this child would have given him anything he wanted, including their own life-sustaining food. Now they are beginning to expect a little giving on his part. But he doesn't want to give. Taking has been his way of life from conception. And this arrangement suits him just fine.

We adults, sensing the capabilities of children, expect them to give-and-take at a level appropriate to their maturity. When they fall behind our expectations, we become irritated. Children NEVER make a smooth transition from the utterly self-centered state to the socially conscious give-and-take.

We are delighted when the three-month-old grabs food from our hand and stuffs it in his mouth, but let a three-year-old try it and it is not so cute. We are delighted when a three-year-old interrupts our conversation with a tale of his own, but a nine-year-old is expected to say "Excuse me" and wait for an appropriate time to participate in the conversation.

When we believe that a child has matured to the point of being capable of responsible action, we automatically expect it of him. If he is slow to assume his duty, we become irritated with him for not "acting his age."

The beasts of the earth, in contrast to man, never need to deny their natural drives. They are within their intended boundaries living for self-gratification. But the growing child or adult who doesn't rise above self-indulging desires has fallen from God's intention and design. The root of all sin is found in the runaway indulgence of God-given desires. Although the child may not have matured to the point of accountability, still, his unrestrained indulgence is the very substance of future sinfulness.

A SPIRITUAL FETUS

Life is designed by God to be a spiritual womb, a place where moral development begins after birth and continues throughout life. The early years after birth could be viewed as the prenatal development of a moral being.

At their creation, Adam and Eve were complete physically, but morally undeveloped. A four-month fetus, still in the mother's womb, is a living soul. Though all of its tiny members match those of a mature adult, it is yet an incomplete creation needing further growth before becoming distinct from its mother. In like manner, a three-year-old child, morally, has all the tiny features of a morally responsible adult— a knowledge of right and wrong, a sense of justice, accountability, conscience, duty, guilt, shame, etc. Yet, none of the moral faculties are developed to the point of being fully operative and independent. The child is not a morally viable soul. He is an incomplete moral being. He is not accountable. Morally, the three-year-old is still in the womb. Moral life begins development sometime after birth, probably in the second or third year, and continues until it matures at about ten to fifteen years of age.

Like physical development in the womb, moral development is a slow transition from no moral understanding at birth to complete accountability at some point in the child's youth. There are vast differences of opinion as to when God holds a child accountable for his own actions and thoughts. From time immemorial, age twelve has been the traditional "age of accountability." But accountability is not an age; it is a state *(James 4:17; Lev. 5:3)*. Biblically, it will be sometime before twenty years of age *(Deut. 1:39* with *Num. 14:29-31)*. Some children may be accountable as early as five, while others may not be fully accountable until nineteen. The mentally impaired may never develop to the point of moral responsibility. But age is not the issue. The point is that moral development is a process, and the small child is not yet a viable moral soul.

THE DILEMMA

The dilemma parents face is this: How do we relate to the child during this transitional period as he progresses from no moral understanding to complete accountability? For example, when a five-year-old child is, say, 30% morally cognizant and 70% morally naive, how does a parent hold the child accountable? We know that God will not condemn a child whose moral faculties are not completely operative, but how do parents determine the degree to which the child should be held responsible? This uncertainty causes many parents to hesitate. But if parents wait until the child can understand the need to exercise self-control before they demand it of him, he will have developed both a history and a habit of indulging his flesh to the fullest. The problem the parent must address is that natural drives are active long before reason. During the years before the child is capable of self-motivated restraint, parents usually assist the child's self-indulgence by providing an environment where little is expected.

PARENTAL RESPONSIBILITY

Here is where we come to the crux of this chapter and the background for this book. It is important to understand: PARENTS MUST ASSUME CONTROL OF THE MORAL DEVELOPMENT OF THEIR CHILDREN. During the early years, we do not want to destroy the child's natural drives, <u>but we must constrain him to exercise self-discipline</u>. The parents' role is not that of policemen, but more like that of the Holy Spirit. When a child has his sails full of wind (strong drives), but no compass (moral discernment), his parents must serve as his navigator. When a child is incapable of holding moral values, parental training and example will be his "standard." <u>Before he can DECIDE to do good, his parents must CONDITION him to do good</u>. There was a time when the child's mother breathed for him, ate for him, and handled his waste. Likewise, in the moral realm, until the child's reason and moral faculties develop to the point of independent operation, parents must be the voice of his fetal conscience. Parents must provide initiative and instill a set of values.

Each day brings the child closer to moral responsibility. Someday his spiritual heart will function without you. He will leave the protection of your sanctification and stand alone in the light of his own conscience *(1 Cor. 7:14)*. Until he matures to that point, the only moderation the child will know is what his parents instill.

Parents must be sensitive to their role in the child's moral development. One day he is going to choose without you. Will he make the right choice? No amount of training is going to override the certainty of sin developing, but the training parents give can lessen the child's addiction to the flesh and make it easier for repentance to follow sinful indulgence.

Parents do not deal with the small child's "selfishness" as sin, but they must be aware that it will soon move in that direction. Drives which are not in themselves evil, nonetheless, form the occasion to sin. As parents train the young child, they must take into consideration the evil that a self-willed spirit will eventually bring.

Parents cannot impart righteousness to their children, but they can help them develop a firm commitment to righteousness. Parents cannot write the law on the hearts of their children, but they can write the law and the gospel on their developing consciences.

Anticipating the child's development, and knowing that evil will come to be a part of his moral nature, places an urgent sense of responsibility upon parents. The world is an undertow pulling children to destruction. Looking at statistics alone, the probability is against their moral survival. The training parents give and the wisdom they impart can make all the difference in the outcome. You hold an eternal soul in your hands. You cannot afford to give in to indifference, laziness, or careless neglect. It is your responsibility to determine what level of understanding your child possesses and to hold him accountable at that level.

This is an almost impossible task if you depend on your intellect alone. If you are the principal caretaker of your child, your heart will be able to discern the world from his perspective. When the child believes it is wrong, it is wrong *(James 4:17)*. Where the child possesses moral understanding, yet disobeys, he should be punished with the rod. Where he does not understand the moral quality of his actions, he should be trained and conditioned.

WHEN DRIVES BECOME SIN

When does this innocent, natural selfishness of a child become sin? In other words, when is a child to blame? Keep in mind that a child will not come under condemnation until his moral faculties are fully operative.

As the child's reason and moral faculties develop, he gradually understands his moral responsibility and duty. At some point (as moral perception grows to a point where he can be held fully accountable), every child faces his own *"tree of knowledge of good and evil." (See Deut. 1:39)* So far, everyone (except Jesus) has "eaten" (personally violated his own God-given understanding of right and wrong), resulting in personal condemnation.

God will not condemn a child until he has grown into a state of accountability. However, during this transition, which occurs between the ages of about two and fourteen, the child's accountability will increase with the growth of his moral awareness. When a child goes against his conscience, however limited and incomplete his understanding may be, he is then guilty. The degree to which his understanding has developed is the degree to which his actions can be called sin. The presence of guilt is a good barometer as to how much his conscience has developed.

Again, though the child may feel guilt in some areas, the responsibility for sin is not imputed unto him until his moral soul is fully functional. An unfinished clock, still in the making, may have moving parts, but it will not keep time until every last piece is properly installed.

WALKING AFTER THE FLESH

All children seem bent toward evil. This propensity to sin is found in the fleshly body seeking selfish gratification. After the child has given himself over to fleshly appetite, Paul labels his flesh as *"sinful flesh (Rom. 8:3),"* that is, flesh "full" of sin. As the body of flesh was the occasion of Eve's sin and the occasion of Christ's temptation, so is it the occasion of your child's development into selfishness—which, at maturity, will constitute sinfulness.

WALKING AFTER THE SPIRIT

Even before a child's conscience is partially operative, he must be trained to practice self-restraint. For if a child is allowed to violate his budding conscience, and continues to do so as he grows to full maturity, he will find himself already fully given over to his flesh long before he begins to develop a sense of duty. Therefore, before moral development begins (at about two years of age), parents must bring the child's flesh into complete subjection.

By the third year and beyond, that part of the child that is awakened to moral duty should be taught to voluntarily surrender to the rule of law. If you allow the flesh to run its natural course, the child will be possessed of many unruly passions and lusts long before he is cognizant enough to assume responsibility.

IN MY HANDS

The clay formed into a vessel of dishonor was marred while in the potter's hand, only to be remade into a vessel of honor fit for the master's table. If God is the potter and your child is the clay, you are the wheel on which the clay is to be turned. As Adam and Eve were given a garden to dress and keep, you have been given loan of a little heart and mind to dress and keep.

There will come a time when your child must stand alone before *"the tree of knowledge of good and evil."* As the purpose of God has permitted, he will inevitably partake of the forbidden fruit. Now, in the developing years, you can make a difference in how he will respond after he has "eaten."

Everything a child experiences, either by way of indulgence or the self-restraint you impose, is preparing him for the day when he will mature into a responsible, moral soul. Somewhere on that road of development, each child will graduate into compete accountability. That child will then stand alone before God, "without excuse."

A DIVINE CALLING

With this understanding, you can better appreciate what is taking place in your developing child. Just as the child Jesus grew in wisdom and knowledge, so your child is going through a growth of understanding. The Holy Scriptures are able to make him *"wise unto salvation (2 Tim. 3:15)."* You must equip your child to save himself from this *"untoward generation (Acts 2:40)."* God has a prototype of the finished product. It is that he might be *"conformed to the image of his Son (Rom. 8:29)."* You must work with God toward the day when your children will be conformed to *"the measure of the stature of the fulness of Christ (Eph. 4:13)."* The promise of God is still operative: *"Train up a child in the way he should go, and when he is old, he will not depart from it (Proverbs 22:6)."*

CHAPTER 3
Parental Anger

NO MORE CHANCES

As I was working on this book, a young mother said to me, "I get so angry sometimes; I treat the children so badly. They just upset me. Johnny is always picking on Mary and making her whine. I have to just stay on top of them all the time to prevent them from doing something they shouldn't. What can I do to overcome my anger?"

Previously, this mother rewarded disobedience by saying, "Now Johnny, I have told you not to do that. I am going to give you one more chance and then I will have to spank you." As he continued to disobey, her frustration mounted.

The mother had effectively taught Johnny that he could disobey until her frustration reached a certain level. When he perceived she had reached her limit, he knew it was time to back off for a while. He could return to his disobedience as soon as she cooled off. Sometimes, miscalculating, he pushed her too far and she would "explode" before he could comply.

This mother could overcome her anger if she would remove the cause. No, not the child—his disobedience. In time, she always got him to obey. There was usually a long, drawn out, tense, and competitive prelude to his eventual obedience. Yet her child was actually responding quite predictably. She had trained him not to obey until her anger reached a certain intensity.

I gave her a copy of this manuscript in its early form. Reading it, she decided to make some changes. She made it plain to her son that he was not to tease his smaller sister. She told Johnny that if he disobeyed he would be spanked for the first offense. The first spanking was a shock to Johnny. Mother was no longer waiting until she got mad. No warnings, no threats—she expected him to obey the very first time!

After two days of Mother rewarding every transgression with a

spanking, Johnny turned to her and said, "But Mother, you are not giving me any more chances!" The mother said, "That's right, you don't get
any more chances. From now on I will expect you to obey the first
time." He had been using his "chances" to purchase disobedience. After
two years, he now obeys the first time, and Mother no longer gets angry.

LICENSE TO DISOBEY

When the State Fish & Game Commission issues permits
allowing you to catch five trout but no more, they are not preventing
trout fishing, they are advocating it. This mother had issued Johnny a
license to be disobedient five times, but punished him for the sixth
offense. So every day he went fishing for trouble, but always with an
eye on the "warden." He would try to anticipate when to stop short of
the real "last chance."

When Mom outlawed disobedience by reducing the "limit" to
zero, little Johnny had to test the lawgiver to see if it was just another
permit. When the "Mother Warden" proved to be serious, he decided
that he didn't love "fishing for trouble" enough to pay the fine for what
he caught. Little Johnny started obeying all laws the first time.

If State Troopers ceased writing speeding tickets and instead
started nagging and threatening, it would be tantamount to abolishing
the speed limit. Picture a trooper pulling a speeder over and then
explaining how sad it makes him feel for them to be going so fast. Can
you see a trooper sitting on the side of the road shaking his fist and turning red in the face as each car sped by? Imagine him pulling a speeder
over for the sixth time and saying, "Now, I am not going to tell you
again!" If this were the case then all law and order would break down
into *"every man did that which was right in his own eyes."*

Most automobile drivers are aware that the radar patrolman
will usually allow motorists to go four miles-per-hour over the speed
limit without issuing a ticket. Consequently, most motorists will drive
four or five miles-per-hour over the speed limit. When you allow your
children to be disobedient four or five times before applying discipline,
you are training them to disobey.

Parent, you can't blame your children if you have trained them
to obey only after several warnings, threats, an ultimatum, and finally a
gesture of force. It's not their fault. It's yours.

ANGER

Parent, have you trained yourself not to discipline immediately but to wait until your irritation builds into anger? If so, then you have allowed anger to be your inducement to discipline. "But how can I stop being so angry?" you ask. It's simple. Don't wait until it becomes a personal affront to you. Discipline immediately upon the slightest disobedience. When children see you motivated by anger and frustration they assume that your "discipline" is just a personal matter, a competition of interest. The child thinks of you as he would another child that is bullying him around. He is not being made to respect the law and the lawgiver. He believes that you are forcing him to give in to superior power. When you act in anger, your child feels that you are committing a personal transgression against him—violating his rights. You have lost the dignity of your office. As they say, "You are not presidential enough." If your child does not see consistency in the lawgiver, in his mind there is no law at all, just competition for supremacy.

You have taught yourself to be motivated only by anger. And you have taught your child to respond only to anger. Having failed to properly train your child, you have allowed the seeds of self-indulgence to grow to ugly proportions.

I MADE A CHILD THAT I DON'T LIKE

The reason you are angry towards your child is that you don't like him. "Oh! I love my child very much." I didn't say you didn't love him. I said there are occasions when you just don't like him, for the simple reason that at such times he is very unlikable. It is impossible to like a whining, selfish, self-centered, spoiled brat.

We cannot help approving of that which is good and lovely, and despising that which is ugly and unwholesome, even in our own flesh and blood. God Himself has such feelings (Ps. 11:5).

You must face the fact that there are times when you just do not like your own child, and for good reason. Many times I have observed parents express what could only be called "intense dislike" for their teenage son or daughter. You may say, "But no one else dislikes them." Yet, if they had to live with them on the same terms as you, they would probably feel the same as you.

But why is your child unlikable? You may not like the answer: You made him that way through your training techniques. You may say, "But, I have not instituted any training techniques. I just scold him when it gets to be too much to bear." Precisely! All children are trained by the responses and actions—or lack of responses and actions—of their principal caretakers. Negative training at its best—or should I say worst—is done by those who, while failing to properly train, try to keep their children in line through threat, intimidation, nagging, anger, and an occasional outburst of spanking.

There is nothing cute or lovable about a whining "brat." To allow a child to whine and disobey is to mold a personality and character that you will eventually find hard to like. By taking control and teaching them to control their emotions and to instantly obey, your children will be cheerful and pleasant. Then you will not only love your children but like them as well. The child reciprocates the parent's delight by loving and honoring them even more. They can both enjoy each other's company. The parents are rested and refreshed by spending time with their children.

THE FOURTEEN-YEAR-OLD

In talking with a mother concerned about the attitude of her fourteen-year-old daughter, it became apparent that she just did not like her own child. The mother's disapproval and frequent criticism had caused the teenager to withdraw and become uncommunicative.

Actually, she was a very good and obedient daughter. She was cheerful with others, but sullen with her mother. The mother was wondering if she should use the rod to correct bad attitudes. She was afraid she had lost all control and influence. The mother had a very stormy youth and was anxious to prevent her daughter from suffering the same fate. The more irritated the mother became and the harder she pushed, the more ground she lost. Sometimes in the areas of talent and personality, parents have narrow expectations for their children and are critical when they fail to measure up to their standards.

I knew this family when their daughter was a child. I recall that even then the mother didn't like her. This mother eventually realized the error of her ways. In taking her own ugly attitude to Christ, she found cleansing and healing. Her daughter quickly showed tremendous improvement.

In reality, when parents are poor trainers, they come to dislike the children they have produced. If you have painted a picture you don't like, don't blame the canvas. Get out the brushes and paint something better over the mess you made.

CHAPTER 4
Tying Strings

MANY STRINGS MAKE STRONG CORDS

There is a mystical bond between caring members of a loving family. I can look at each of my children and feel that union. It is as if we were joined by many strings of mutual love, respect, honor, and all the good times that we have had together.

When two or more people are living together, their interests, opinions, and liberties sometimes clash. Selfishness, indifference, pride, and self-will often cut the strings that unite. When there is not a constant tying of new strings, family members soon find themselves separated by suspicion, distrust, and criticism. The gap can grow so wide that family members become virtual enemies. When this happens between parent and child, it is a serious crisis. Unless new strings are tied, the two will increasingly grow apart. When a teenager says something like, "My parents don't understand me," or "They don't care," it is testimony of a complete cutting of all strings.

PAPER HEARTS

Recently, a father told us of a victory in this area. His first-grader came home from school and occupied himself drawing and cutting out paper hearts. The father and son were close and often did things together. Yet in one thoughtless and insensitive moment, the father lightly poked fun at his son's activity. The child didn't see anything amusing. He turned away and continued his labor of love. Over the next several days the boy concealed his endeavors from his father. The father became aware that a confidence crisis had occurred. The child was withdrawn and resisted all overtures to fellowship. The strings had been cut.

If, at this point, the father had accepted this wall as just a "stage"—or worse, had become irritated and contributed further to the breach—this would have been the beginning of a rift that would have grown wider with the years. But the father was wise and took positive action. After school one day, he said to his son, "Hey, Jessie, you want to go out to the shop with me? We will cut out wooden hearts." Jesse reservedly looked up and seemed to be cautiously analyzing his father's intent. After a moment, his facial expressions changed to believing delight, and he said, "Sure, Dad, that would be great." As they worked together creating a wooden heart for Jesse to give to his friend, the wall came down and camaraderie was restored.

It is important that sons and daughters be able to trust their parents with personal, intimate knowledge. If there is a barrier in this area, when the time comes that they need counsel, to whom shall they go? The feelings of a child are just as important and sacred as are those of an adult. Always treat your children with respect. Never ridicule, mock, or laugh at your child's ideas, creations, or ambitions. The trust you desire to have when they are older must be established and maintained when they are young. If you have an older child with whom you have failed in this area, it is not too late to apologize and reestablish that trust. It may take a while to earn their confidence, but it can be done.

CUT STRINGS

I would say that most parents have allowed the strings that unite them to their children to be cut, and they have not made a responsible effort to tie new ones. It is critical that you take care in this area. When the strings are all cut, you cannot be effective in discipline or training. Without that mutual respect and honor, further discipline only angers and embitters the child.

I talk with many parents who have lost contact with their children. For every one occasion that they tie strings, there are more occasions which cut them. Not only is there no longer a bond, but there is a cloud between them. The parent takes the child's withdrawal and resentment as rebellion (which it is) and fights back with tongue and rod. Like a wild animal, the child further withdraws into his own world of suspicion and distrust.

Similar to the control of a warden over his prisoners, the rod can force outward compliance, but it will not mold character or tie strings of fellowship. The parent feels the child slipping away, sometimes into the fellowship of bad habits or undesirable company. The parent's anger and rejection will never stitch up the breach.

Parents who set aside the rod and resort to sympathy tactics ("If you loved me," or "You hurt me so much," or "Why do you do this to me?") may elicit token compliance, but will only cause the child to yearn for the day when he or she can get away and be free. Many parents have thus driven their young daughter into the arms of an unwholesome lover, or caused their son to move out.

Parents often develop adversarial relationships with their child and are not concerned about it because the child doesn't possess the means to manifest his hurt. By the time parents are forced to admit there is a problem, there is a war zone of obstacles between them. What a child is at four he will be at fourteen, only magnified many times over. Your two-year-old whiner will be a twelve-year-old whiner. The intemperate five-year-old will be an intemperate fifteen-year-old.

STRINGS LEFT UNTIED

A mother came to us concerned for her fourteen-year-old daughter. She had been reared in a very protected environment and was outwardly obedient, but her parents felt there was a breach in the family ties. When given a chore, the girl would obey, but with a sullen attitude. It seemed to this mother that her daughter was tolerating her family but was not at all pleased with their company. There were periods of withdrawal. She seemed to have her own little world. With no outward disobedience, there was nothing for which to reprimand her. This mother had lost fellowship with her daughter. The strings had been cut long ago. Rebuke or discipline would be fruitless, even harmful, until the strings of mutual respect and trust were retied.

THE THREE-YEAR-OLD TRUCKER

As my wife sat talking to a friend, an altercation developed between the young mother's two sons, ages one and three. They both began to scream while tugging at opposite ends of the same toy truck. The mother hollered, "What is wrong with you two?" "He is trying to take my truck," cried the older of the two. "Billy, give Johnny back his truck," she yelled. After further peace-shattering threats and screams of protest, he reluctantly handed over the truck.

The younger child then dejectedly left the yard and stumbled into the house to stand beside his mother—thus punishing the other brother by depriving him of his company. This is an adult form of retribution that children quickly learn.

After the chastisement of loneliness had done its work, the older brother became repentant. Retrieving his truck from the sand pile, he made his way into the house where he found the offended younger brother now sitting in his mother's lap being consoled for his losses on the battlefield. With a smile of reconciliation, the older brother held out the truck to his brother. As the younger brother was about to accept the sacrificial peace offering, the mother turned to see the grinning child dribbling sand from his truck onto the floor. "Get that thing out of here!" she commanded.

The mother was engrossed in her company and failed to regard her children as human beings with complex feelings. She just saw another cleaning job added to her burden.

At this point a psychological transformation occurred in the child. He had just experienced a "repentance" that had cleansed him of anger and selfishness. Weighing his right to possess the truck against his brother's company, he had found that he valued his brother more. He was learning important social lessons about give-and-take. He was learning to share and how to control his possessiveness. His heart was surrendered and vulnerable. He had gone the second mile. Yet when he got to the end of it, he was shocked to find that no one cared. It really didn't matter. He had laid down his guns and was now being fired upon. If they were not going to allow him to surrender, if they didn't care enough to accept his offering, he was not going to stand there exposed, grinning like a fool, while being unjustly blasted.

He didn't understand what the fray was all about. Who could be upset about a little sand on the floor? After all, he had been playing in sand all morning—he loved it. As he studied his mother's threatening face, you could see the little mental wheels turning.

Immediately his smile was replaced by wonder, then puzzlement, and finally, defiance. On his face I saw a devious idea hatched. Knowing that sand on the floor was what stole his show and made her angry, he raised his truck to examine it, and then defiantly dumped the full contents onto the floor. To his satisfaction, it worked. She came apart. She had hurt him and he had successfully retaliated. "Just look at her red face. That will teach her to attack me. Boy, I won this round."

This mother had missed the opportunity to accept the surrender of this rebel leader. Instead she had driven him back into the countryside to practice his civil dissent in defiance of the established authority. Like many rebels, he had no alternate plans for the future. He lived to be a rebel because of his hatred for the authority that he hoped to punish for perceived injustices.

Now, you may think that I am over-dramatizing the child's feelings. It is true that he could not tell you what he was thinking. But this three-year-old child demonstrated that he had a root of bitterness producing his rebellion.

If the parents don't change, by the time the boy becomes a teenager they will throw up their hands and say, "I don't understand that boy. We have taught him right from wrong, taken him to church, and given him what he wants, but he acts like we are the enemy. We have done our best. It is up to the good Lord now."

This mother is failing to tie strings of common respect. The seeds sown at two years will bear fruit at fourteen.

PROBLEM PARENTS

Parent, if you are having problems with your children, just know that you are not alone. Your children are also having problems with you. You are going to have to make adjustments in your own life if you are going to help them. Since you are reading this book, and not your children, and since you are the more experienced of the two, and since God didn't say, "Children, train up your parents," the responsibility is completely yours.

CUTTING STRINGS

I remember looking into the face of one of my boys, knowing that I had cut the strings of trust and fellowship. It was disturbing to see him slip from the mooring and drift away. At the time I had not formulated the terminology, nor even recognized the principle, but I could see that there was a breach. The fault-line was widening. The fault was mine. I had pushed him too hard, demanded too much, and then been critical when he had not performed to my expectations. When, like a turtle, he withdrew into his shell, I could see that he had dismissed me. He had decided to live without me. There was too much pain associated with his father.

I didn't know how to define it, but being fully responsible for his training, I knew that it was my responsibility. I immediately apologized, lightened up, revised my criticism, found the good in what he had done, and suggested an exciting outing. It took me several days of being sensible, fair, just, and kind to completely restore the strings of fellowship. He quickly forgave, and we were restored, once the strings were retied.

GOD HELP THE FATHERS

"And, ye fathers, provoke not your children to wrath: but bring them up in the nurture and admonition of the Lord (Eph. 6:4)." A father who teases his children until they are angry can expect them to do the same to others smaller than themselves. On more than one occasion when scuffling with my boys, I have found myself having fun at their expense (That was when I was bigger than they were). They reminded me to play by the same rules to which they were bound.

Don't laugh this off, fathers. If you make your little boy mad while you are having fun, you are creating a bully. After all, weren't you bullying him? The wrath you provoked in him will be stored up until he can release it on one weaker than himself. That wrath can only be put away if he forgives you. And he cannot forgive until he sees your repentance.

If your child has a root of bitterness, you have a healing ministry to perform. Your heart and life must be fully surrendered to God, or you are wasting your time. You will just have to try to stay out of his way. He will be rearing himself. His chances are not good, but don't increase his bitterness by playing the hypocrite. It is hard enough to make it in this godless world when you have good support. For a kid filled with bitterness and facing it alone, there is not much hope. Maybe his mother can make a difference. Often a boy just shuts out a father for whom he has only disdain, and so relates to his mother in a manner that may allow him to grow up normal.

Father, if you care for your child's soul more than your pride, then humble yourself and ask his forgiveness (even if he is just two years old). Then become a patient father and husband. Spend time with your child doing things that are creative—that gives him a sense of great adventure or accomplishment. You can't lead your child closer to God, peace, and discipline than you are yourself.

WHAT CAN I DO NOW?

Tie some strings. You must be knit together with your child before you can train him. Confess your failure to God and to your child. Ask your child to forgive you for anger and indifference. At first he will suspect it is just a manipulative ploy on your part and will keep his distance. But when he sees that you are sincere, he will respond with forgiveness. Begin the rebuilding process immediately.

Don't barge in and overpower your children with emotion or a new philosophy. Be a friend. Do things with them that they enjoy. Show interest in things that interest them. Be more ready with your ears than with your mouth. Be very sensitive to their concerns. Tie strings until you have earned their respect and honor. If they sense that you like and enjoy them, they will respond in kind. When they like you, they will want to please you, and will be open to your discipline.

The strongest cord of discipline is not found in the whip; rather, it is the weaving together of the strings of mutual love, respect, honor, loyalty, admiration, and caring. It is the difference in being "led by the spirit" and being "under the works of the law." The law gives us direction, but only the spirit of grace gives us power. If you will cultivate fellowship with your child, you will have such cooperation and compliance that you will forget where you last left the rod.

WALKING IN THE FATHER'S LIGHT

I can remember an incident that occurred when I was only four years old. Several of us young kids, about the same age, were walking along behind a row of houses when one of them suggested that we throw rocks at a basement window.

I can still remember my thought process. As I considered doing it, I saw my daddy's face. He never told me not to break windows, but I knew he wouldn't be pleased. I had no law to go by, but I had my father's presence to guide me. It was not the fear of punishment or scolding that motivated me. It was the fear of losing fellowship with my father that led me in the path of righteousness. To please him and enjoy his favor was my strongest impulse. I withdrew from the window-breaking party and walked in my father's light.

My father was not perfect. He wasn't even the best of Christians, but I was not yet aware of that at four, or even ten years of age. To me he was law and grace. As I grew older, I slowly (sometimes with a jolt) came to see him as just another struggling member of the human race. Still, I never outgrew that desire to please him.

As my confidence in him waned, my confidence in God grew. With the eventual transfer of my faith to God (as it should be), I found myself still motivated not by the law and a fear of hell, but by the face of my Heavenly Father. Today, I have a doubly lighted path.

Parent, above all, you must cultivate this kind of a relationship with your child. It is a painful thing to sin against your best buddy. If you can maintain this kind of bond with your children, you will never have a problem child. Deb and I raised five children with none of them ever rebelling against our authority.

SEEING GOD IN DADDY AND MAMMA

When a child is young, his parents are the only "god" he knows. As he awakens to Divine realities, it is through his earthly father that he understands his heavenly Father. Fathers (and mothers also), you are the window through which your young child understands God. A child learns of the character of God through observing his parents. Parents don't have to be perfect, just a balanced representation of God's personality. Everything that God is in character and government, parents should display within the limits of their humanity. Parents need not be all-powerful, just the child's source of strength. They don't have to be all-wise, just wise enough to guide the child and warrant admiration. Parents need not be sinless, just demonstrate a commitment to goodness. As a child sees his parents' humble dependence on and love for God, because he loves and respects his parents, he will love and honor the One his parents love.

As the child relates to the figurehead of parental authority, in like manner he will later be prone to relate to God. If parents allow their commands to be treated lightly, the child will take the commandments of God lightly also.

On the other extreme, children with cruel fathers usually mature with a foreboding of their heavenly Father, whereas those disciplined to lovingly obey their earthly fathers are more ready to obey their heavenly Father.

YOU CAN TIE STRINGS

If you sense that the strings of fellowship have been cut, you will want to tie new ones. Here are just a few suggestions on tying strings:

- First and foremost, look at your children with pleasure and smile.
- Enjoy their company and demonstrate it by inviting them to go with you when the only reason is a desire to have them with you. For the young, look at pictures or read a book together.
- Sit on the floor and play. Tumble and roll, laugh, and tickle.
- Take them on outings of adventure, excitement, and "danger."
- Take a ten-minute trip to the tree house to see their creations.

- Let them lead you out to the swing to show off their latest stunt.

- Make a kite or build a birdhouse together.

- Mother, teach your children to do everything that must be done in the house. Make it a fun experience. Don't use the very young as slave labor, or they will experience burnout. Let them bake cookies at three years of age. When you are sewing, let the young ones sit on the floor and cut out doll clothes. When you are painting, let them make a few swipes.

- Fathers, involve your sons in the manly role of protector and provider. If they can walk, they can carry in groceries or bring in firewood. Brag on their achievements.

The idea is for them to feel that they are very special to you, and for them to know that you find great satisfaction and delight in sharing with them. If you order your life so your children feel needed, they will desire to walk in harmony with you.

CHAPTER 5

The Rod

"I LOVE MY BABY TOO MUCH TO SPANK HIM"

I observed a mother vainly trying to get her discontent child to obey a simple command, but he was too preoccupied with his complaining, whining, and anger. The little tyrant's rebellious antics left the mother miserable and ill tempered. She continued to plead with him as if she was trying to remember what she learned about "positive affirmation" and not "stifling his personal expression."

As an objective observer, concerned only for the child's happiness and well being, I said to the mother, "Why don't you give him a spanking and make him happy?" In shock, she replied, "Oh, he will grow out of it. It's just a stage he is going through."

If she truly believes that this is just a natural stage (a condition for which little Johnny is not responsible), why does she become enraged at times, demanding a different conduct or attitude? This mother, while excusing him and maintaining a "patient" vigil for the "stage" to run its course, and in spite of her verbalized philosophy, does blame the child. Down inside, she knows he should be—could be—decidedly different. The criticism and rejection he feels from his disapproving mother and from the public in general sets him against authority.

We have progressed to the place where a discussion of the use of the rod is in order. Let's talk about spankings—sometimes called "whippings." *"He that spareth his rod hateth his son: but he that loveth him chasteneth him betimes (Prov. 13:24)."* What God says goes exactly opposite to the feelings of many parents and educators. The passage clearly states that a failure to apply the rod is due to the parents hating the child. "No!" cries a mother, "I love my child too much to spank him." The parent who responds thus does not understand: 1) the authority of God's word, 2) the nature of love, 3) his (or her) own feelings, 4) the character of God, 5) the needs of the child.

1. Understanding the authority of God's Word

The same God who said: *"Suffer the little children to come unto me, and forbid them not... (Mark 10:14),"* also said:

• *"Chasten thy son while there is hope, and let not thy soul spare for his crying (Prov. 19:18)."*

• *"He that spareth his rod hateth his son: but he that loveth him chasteneth him betimes (Prov. 13:24)."*

• *"Foolishness is bound in the heart of a child; but the rod of correction shall drive it far from him (Prov. 22:15)."*

• *"Withhold not correction from the child: for if thou beatest him with the rod, he shall not die. Thou shalt beat him with the rod, and shalt deliver his soul from hell (Prov. 23:13-14)."*

• *"The rod and reproof give wisdom: but a child left to himself bringeth his mother to shame (Prov. 29:15)."*

• *"Correct thy son, and he shall give thee rest; yea, he shall give delight unto thy soul (Prov. 29: 17)."*

2. Understanding the nature of love

You may have strong feelings that prevent you from spanking your child, but it is not love. The God who made little children, and therefore knows what is best for them, has told parents to employ the rod in training up their children. To refrain from doing so, based on a claim of love, is an indictment against God Himself. Your actions assume that either God does not desire what is best for your child or you know better than He.

Parent, you must recognize the difference between true love and sentiment. Natural human sentiment—often taken to be love—can be harmful if not submitted to wisdom. Love is not sentiment. That is, love is not the deep feelings we often have in association with those close to us. Such feelings can be, and often are, self serving.

Love is not an emotion at all. Love, in the purest sense, is goodwill toward and good doing for your fellow man. True love is disinterested. That is, there is no thought of personal gain or of personal loss in the act of loving.

3. Understanding one's own feelings

An emotionally weak mother often looks to her child's clinging dependence for her own self-fulfillment. She finds a deep need met within her as she constantly dotes over the infant's every want. Her consuming passion for the child, which she takes to be love, is too sacred for her to jeopardize by spanking the child. Her insecurity causes her to consider only what she perceives to be her loss in the act of spanking. She is afraid to do anything that might cause the child to reject her. She is not motivated by love for the child, but by self-love. Her own emotional weakness takes precedence over the child's needs.

The pitiful look of betrayal in his poor little eyes just breaks her suffering heart. It would hurt her too much to obey God in training up her child. Because of her fear of personal, emotional suffering, she neglects the rod. *"He that spareth his rod hateth his son: but he that loveth him chasteneth him betimes (Prov. 13:24)."*

In her own need, she is so naive as to believe that her "sweet" child will grow out of it and become a wonderful person. She thinks, "Just give him more love and a little more time; he doesn't understand yet." True love is ignoring your needs and doing what is good for the child. If a mother should smother her baby while kissing him, she has not loved him.

Her own anger may cause her to distrust her motives in corporal punishment. (See chapter 3, PARENTAL ANGER.) Then again, her fears may go back to the memory of a tyrannical, unreasonable father. She may have vowed, "I will never be like my father. I will love my children. They will not fear me the way I feared my father." The father not only hurt her, he is now hurting her children by causing her to react in the opposite extreme.

Sometimes images from the past cause a mother to have deep foreboding every time the father spanks the children. Mothers who have been conditioned to associate anger with discipline impute a motive of anger to anyone who spanks a child. The child perceives the protectiveness of the mother and will whine for her when the father attempts to discipline. When the father does discipline the child, the kid's knowledge that she is not in agreement prevents it from being effective and causes deviousness in the child. It is time to stop reacting to the past and start acting as God and sound reason dictate.

Some parents fail to use the rod because of peer pressure. They may be in disagreement with their own parents about child training. The modern parent is bombarded with propaganda, supposedly based on the latest psychological research, which villainizes Biblically based child rearing. Parents are shamed and must look over their shoulders before applying discipline.

4. Understanding the character of God

The parent who excuses himself from using the rod based on an excuse of loving the child too much does not understand the character and methods of God toward His own people.

There is a twisted perspective that has edged into Christian thinking. It goes something like this: "Since God is love, He is not discriminating, demanding, vindictive, or vengeful." Essentially, they view the love of God as incompatible with the justice of God. It seems to them that He must be either one or the other. There is a vague, undefined sense that God was once vengeful, but is now passive, tolerant, and ecumenical—the Universal Father. God is stripped of His balanced personality and defined in a non-threatening way. Heaven is well received; hell is suspect. *"Judge not,"* the most popular verse in the Bible, is quoted as if God Himself could no longer discriminate between right and wrong.

As much as God is love, He is also holy, just, and true. It is out of His love of righteousness that He is coming in *"flaming fire taking vengeance on them that know not God, and that obey not the gospel of our Lord Jesus Christ (2 Thes. 1:8)."* To choose one side of God's character as a model for our actions while rejecting the other can hardly be called a virtue.

God spanks His children

Those who excuse themselves from using the rod by claiming that their actions are more righteous are, by inference, condemning God. *"For whom the Lord loveth he chasteneth, and scourgeth every son whom he receiveth. If ye endure chastening, God dealeth with you as with sons; for what son is he whom the father chasteneth not? But if ye be without chastisement, whereof all are partakers, then are ye bastards, and not sons (Heb. 12:6-8)."*

Then it says He chastens us *"for our own profit, that we might be partakers of his holiness (Heb. 12:10)."* This is a most profound statement! God does not have any sons who escape chastisement—*"all are partakers."* And did He stop loving those whom he chastened? Quite the contrary, love was His motivation for the "spanking." Only through chastisement could His sons fully partake of His holiness. He does it *"for our own profit."*

"No chastening for the present seemeth to be joyous, but grievous... (Heb. 12:11)." God's chastisement is a painful "whipping." Our

"fathers of the flesh...chastened us after their own pleasure... (Heb. 12: 9, 10)." The Scripture not only condones physical *"scourging,"* but promotes it as a means to holiness—when administered for the son's *"profit."*

The chastisement is represented as a sure sign of love: *"for whom the Lord loveth, he chasteneth."* If one is not chastened, it is not only an indication of not being loved, but of being a *"bastard."* So we see that it is God's love for us that motivates His acts of chastisement. Thus, our original passage in *Prov. 13:24, "He that spareth his rod hateth his son: but he that loveth him chasteneth him betimes."*

If God's love is expressed by the "whippings" He gives, then can we not love our children enough to chasten them unto holiness? I heard a rebellious teenager say, "If they only loved me enough to whip me."

Recently, a mother told us that after cracking down on her children with consistent use of the rod, one child thanked God for making his mama sweeter. The increased spankings had reduced disobedience, causing the child to be more in harmony with his mother. He interpreted this to be a sweeter mother, for three spankings a day are much less stressful than fifty scowls of disapproval.

5. Understanding the needs of the child

The very nature of the child makes the rod an indispensable element in child training and discipline. We will summarize the previous comments on the nature of a child (chapter 2) and then draw some important practical applications.

SUMMARY: *"They go astray as soon as they be born, speaking lies (Psalm 58:3)."* An infant has real needs for food, cuddling, and bodily comfort. But he soon learns that by falsely representing his needs he can get his wants met as well. He is in the first stages of runaway indulgence. But due to the immaturity of his soul, God does not count his lies as sin. *"Therefore to him that knoweth to do good, and doeth it not, to him it is sin (James 4:17). Sin is not imputed where there is no law (Rom. 5:13)."* The infant, not knowing *"good and evil (Deut. 1:39),"* is not held responsible for his lack of conformity to the law. Nevertheless, infants do lie about their condition and needs. And children issue forth with a multitude of other selfishly motivated thoughts and acts that will, upon their growing into the *"knowledge of good and evil,"* constitute a *"body of sin."* Though they are not now to blame, as their moral understanding matures, their consciences will be awakened and they will be held accountable.

Your child is in a body of infirm flesh. The God-given drives toward the fulfillment of bodily needs and appetites form a constant and incessant occasion to lust. The drive itself is not sin. Lust of the flesh is natural *(Deut. 12:15)*. But when one is *"drawn away of his own lust, and enticed,"* and the lust conceives with opportunity, *"...it bringeth forth sin (James 1:14,15)."*

You cannot prevent your child from the life of testing that his body of flesh will bring, but you can train him in self-denial so that he will not develop habits of selfish indulgence. The rod is your divine enforcer. *"The rod and reproof give wisdom... (Prov. 29:15)."*

Understand that we are not suggesting that a child can be trained into the Christian experience, only that his mind and body should be developed to their highest possible natural discipline. By elevating his standards and causing him to value truth and purity, you are aiding the Spirit in convicting him of sin, which, in time, will cause him to realize his need for a Savior. This is the lawful use of the law.

NEGATIVE FEELINGS

Understanding the development of a child helps us to understand our role in training. Self-indulgence and an unruled spirit will produce emotional dissatisfaction in children—adults as well. An undisciplined child will be insecure. Lack of self-control results in anger. A failure to get one's own way causes self-pity. Unfulfilled lust causes restless agitation. Feelings of being treated unfairly precipitate bitterness. For these reasons both the child and the adult have an innate need to be governed. We were created to be under government. It is in our human nature. Otherwise purposelessness and lack of identity will result. *"A child left to himself bringeth his mother to shame (Prov. 9:15)."*

INTIMIDATION

The average parental response to a disobedient child is to lecture him, shame him, or deprive him of some privilege. His parents may make him go to his room or sit in a corner, or jerk him around and administer a few hasty slaps. Finally they top it off with a threat and dismiss him with a scowl. A child thus denigrated will not be released from his guilt or rebellion. On the contrary, it will only provoke him to react in anger and make excuses. Accusations, threats, and ridicule, which are intimidation, may cause the child to yield temporary compliance, but his heart of uncleanness remains, and his self-image degrades. He may fall into a pattern commonly labeled "self-loathing."

GUILT AND SELF-LOATHING

The smallest child, who knows he has failed in doing what he ought, suffers guilt. Guilt is involuntary self-accusation. It is the soul knowing itself and not liking what it sees. Although the child's soulish faculties are not yet completely operative, nonetheless, a child who violates his budding conscience becomes burdened with guilt and, if left unattended, self-loathing.

In the extraordinary ignorance of modern psychology, many entertain the assumption that man's major problem is "not loving himself." This comes from a failure to understand the association of the emotion of self-loathing, which comes from guilt, with the supreme motivation of self-love. Taking their cue from secular "wisdom," misguided parents try to build up their child's self-image through "positive affirmation." It is nauseating to see parents trying to purge their children of guilt with empty, sweet words.

No one needs to be encouraged to love himself. By creation, we naturally love ourselves. We think in terms of what will benefit us. *"For no man ever yet hateth his flesh; but nourisheth and cherisheth it (Eph. 5:29)."*

By nature, every human values righteousness and expects it of himself. To fail to live up to your own standards results in self-condemnation and guilt. The human spirit, given by God, comes equipped with a resident, divine judge—the conscience. The conscience is nothing more than the mind knowing itself.

The higher one values his own good (loves himself), the greater his own despising (which is guilt) when he fails to achieve his goals of doing right. The subsequent self-loathing is nothing but self-rebuke for failure to benefit the person he loves the most—HIMSELF.

A child or adult who is self-loathing is one whose conscience is condemning the self for not living up to the ideals of self-love. Self-loathing is based on self-love. The more one loves himself, the deeper the self-loathing. If one truly hated himself, he would find great satisfaction in his own failures. When a child is self-loathing, he is damning himself for known violations of conscience and for his failure to live up to his own standards. No child can be led from the pit of self-condemnation by pouring empty praise on him. He knows better.

GUILT

Guilt only occurs when one honestly judges himself to be worthy of blame. One may inappropriately be convinced of blame, but guilt is nonetheless self-incrimination for perceived wrongdoing. Bad behavior causes guilt. So does rejection and ridicule, if the child becomes convinced that he is the one in the wrong.

Emotionally unstable parents sometimes use guilt to manipulate their children. Parents who try to shame or humiliate their children into right behavior may see the child temporarily acquiesce. But obedience performed out of the desperation of guilt only deepens guilt, putting the child further out of touch with true repentance and healing.

Guilt is never in itself restorative. That is, it does not tend toward less blameworthy actions. On the contrary, the guilty soul is a slave to every temptation. Guilt puts one out of touch with normal psychological restraints. The despair of guilt abolishes motivation to do right. The anguish of failure lowers one's expectations of self. Guilt lowers self-esteem to the point where one does not expect to do other than fail.

This reality has caused modern psychologists to view guilt itself as the culprit. To address guilt as if it were the disease is like dealing with the pain of a toothache but not the tooth.

Guilt is an essential part of our natural, moral self. Without it we would be like a smoke detector with no alarm. But, guilt is only a means to an end, a temporary condition. It's the soul's pain, as when we touch something hot, designed to give us warning, to change our actions. It is a great blessing to feel genuine guilt, a sign of life, a healthy response.

Guilty souls who are resigned to their condition are often seen inflicting pain and suffering upon themselves. This self-abuse is an unconscious attempt to "pay the fiddler." The conscience is indelibly imprinted with a conviction that sin deserves punishment. We intuitively know that wrongdoing not only deserves but will one day face punishment. From the earliest awakenings of conscience a child is in the grip of this reality. It remains a basic presupposition of life.

Guilt is the law's chief witness against the sinner. If guilt is not resolved, it will shackle the damned in the eternal misery of their sins. Like a zealous prosecuting attorney, the conscience will not drop its case until it is sure that justice has been done. A guilty soul is a soul that feels it deserves punishment equal to the offense. This is a psychological reality. The guilt-burdened soul cries out for the lashes and nails of justice. That is why the soul of man never rests until the conscience has been purged by a believing look at the bleeding, crucified Lamb of God.

Christians find release from their guilt through the Savior who suffered the curse of their sins, but their children cannot yet understand that the Creator has been lashed and nailed in their place. Yet, parents need not wait until their children are old enough to understand the vicarious death of Christ to purge their children of guilt. God has provided parents with a tool to cleanse their children of guilt—the rod of correction.

I observed a small child who, upon being caught in a misdeed, turned her backside to her parents, pulled her diaper down, and gave herself three slaps on the bare bottom. The offering, though cute, was not accepted. The lawgiver must administer this kind of chastisement in order to effectively remove guilt. A child knows but one lawgiver—his parents.

Do not follow the modern philosophy of trying to eliminate guilt by fudging on the standards or by pumping the guilty child up with false worth. Keep the standards high—as high as the person of Christ. Let the guilt come, and while the child is yet too young to understand, purge his guilt by means of the rod. When understanding finally comes, he will readily grasp the principles of the cross.

THE POWER OF "ABSOLUTION"

Parents hold in their hands (in the form of a little switch) the power to absolve the child of guilt, cleanse his soul, instruct his spirit, strengthen his resolve, and give him a fresh start through a confidence that all indebtedness is paid. *"The blueness of a wound cleanseth away evil: so do stripes the inward parts of the belly (Prov. 20:30)."* *"Inward parts of the belly"* is a description of the physical sensations associated with guilt.

Stripes *("scourgeth" Heb. 12:6)* are said to be to the soul what the healing blood flow is to a wound. A child properly and timely spanked is healed in the soul and restored to wholeness of spirit. A child can be turned back from the road to hell through proper spankings. *"Withhold not correction from the child: for if thou beatest him with the rod, he shall not die. Thou shalt beat him with the rod, and shalt deliver his soul from hell (Prov. 23:13,14)."*

Father, as high priest of the family you can reconcile your child to newness of life. Guilt gives Satan a just calling card and a door of access to your child. In conjunction with teaching, the properly administered spanking is restorative as nothing else can be.

A spanking (whipping, paddling, switching, or belting) is indispensable to the removal of guilt in your child. His very conscience (nature) demands punishment.

COMFORTING ROD

Do you comfort your child with the rod? If you have not seen the rod as a comfort to your child, you have missed its purpose. *"Thy rod and thy staff they comfort me (Psalm 23:4).)" "I will chasten him with the rod...(2 Sam. 7:14)." "Then will I visit their transgression with the rod, and their iniquities with stripes (Psalm 89:32)."*

David, who experienced the rod of God's correction and was chastened for transgression, found comfort in the Divine discipline. The rod was a comfort to him. It assured him of God's control, concern, love, and commitment. Children need to know that someone is in control.

"Chasten thy son while there is hope, and let not thy soul spare for his crying (Prov. 19:18)." Proper use of the rod gives new hope to a rebellious child. Parents are exhorted to not allow the child's crying to cause them to lighten up on the intensity or duration of the spanking. Parents' emotions can stand in the way of a thorough cleansing.

An unchastened child is not only restless and irritable in his own spirit, but causes the whole house to be in turmoil. *"Correct thy son, and he shall give thee rest; yea, he shall give delight unto thy soul (Prov. 29:17)."*

THERE WAS A MIRACLE HERE TONIGHT

Recently, a young couple with five children came to us for advice. The wife had become unresponsive to her husband and irritable with their three children under five. "I sometimes feel like I am going crazy. I don't want to have any more children," she blurted out.

They stayed in our home for a couple of days, submitting to scrutiny. After a little instruction about consistent training and the proper use of the rod they went home and gave it a try. Two weeks later they were in a church meeting where I was speaking. Their children all sat on the bench with them, never making a stir. Afterward, the father, eyes filled with wonder, exclaimed, "There was a miracle here tonight and no one seemed to notice." As I was looking around for discarded crutches, he continued, "A whole service and not a peep! I can't believe it!" A little training and a little discipline with the rod, and the children gave them "rest" and "delight." Furthermore, the children were obviously happier. The mother later said, "Now, I think I would like to have more children."

THE MAGIC WAND

Don't think of the rod as a weapon of defense or a show of force, think of it as a "magic wand." The first time parents see its restorative powers they are amazed. I still marvel at the power of the little rod.

Picture a child of any age who is miserable, complaining, and a bully to other kids. When you look at him, all you see is the inside of a bottom lip. Every device has failed to bring relief. The kid feels that he is living in foreign, occupied territory. He is obviously plotting the day when he will throw off his yoke of bondage. Bribed, threatened, or swatted, he only gets worse. Fail to use the rod on this child, and you are creating a "Nazi." After a short explanation about bad attitudes and the need to love, patiently and calmly apply the rod to his backside. Somehow, after eight or ten licks, the poison is transformed into gushing love and contentment. The world becomes a beautiful place. A brand new child emerges. It makes an adult stare at the rod in wonder, trying to see what magic is contained therein. God would not have commanded parents to use the rod if it was not good for the child.

THE CANE, NOT THE CORNER

I know of one young boy that is not spanked when he throws a tantrum or disobeys. It seems that he delights in doing what he is commanded not to do. The more he rebels, the meaner and guiltier he gets. For punishment he is pinched or made to sit in the corner, or sometimes put in a dark closet. When he comes out, he is madder than ever. He could intimidate a fire-eating dragon.

Sitting in a corner, he was heard to say, "Nobody likes me. I'm as bad as the Devil. I never do anything right." This little fellow is being reared to take his place in a jail cell. Dark corners and dark closets breed darkness in the soul. An empty room and a pouting child incubate guilt and anger. Only the rod and reproof bring correction. Somehow children know the rod is their just due.

The rod is a gift from God; use it as the hand of God to train your children.

CHAPTER 6
Applying the Rod

TO DO MY DUTY

When the time comes to apply the rod, take a deep breath, relax, and pray, "Lord, make this a valuable learning session. Cleanse my child of ill temper and rebellion. May I properly represent your cause in this matter." Don't be hasty or raise your voice. The child should be able to anticipate the coming rod by your utterly calm and controlled spirit.

At this point he will panic and rush to demonstrate obedience. Never reward delayed obedience by suspending the sentence. And unless all else fails, don't drag him to the place of cleansing. Part of his training is to come submissively. However, if you are just beginning to institute training on an already rebellious child that runs from discipline, and he is too incoherent to listen, then use whatever force is necessary to bring him to bay. If you have to sit on him to spank him, then do not hesitate. And hold him there until he has surrendered. Prove that you are bigger, tougher, more patiently enduring, and are unmoved by his wailing. Defeat him totally. Accept no conditions for surrender—no compromise. You are to rule over him as a benevolent sovereign. Your word is final.

When you administer the rod, tell him to bend over on the bed or couch. While he is in this position, admonish him—you have his undivided attention. Slowly begin to spank. If you go too fast, you may not allow time enough for the inner transformation to occur.

Use your own judgment as to what is effective. I have found five to ten licks are usually sufficient. As the child gets older, the licks must become more forceful if the experience is going to be effective in purging his rebellion. A general rule is to continue the disciplinary action until the child has surrendered. A spanking is made effective, not by its severity, but by its certainty. Spankings don't have to be as hard when they are consistently applied. Your calm dignity will set the stage to make it more effective.

If an older child perceives a self-defensive, competitive posture in his parent, he will react to the spanking much as he would if whipped by an older, bigger boy down the road. He will become subdued and cautious, but not honoring. It may control his actions, but it will not change his attitude.

INSTRUMENTS OF LOVE

Make it a point never to use your hand for spanking. Exceptions should be highly justified. It is usually the impatient, personally offended parent whose hand continually darts out like a snake. The parent, too busy to take the time needed for training, blurts out, "Just get off my back, leave me alone, stop bothering me." The hand swatting is a release of the parent's own frustration.

Furthermore, where the child is concerned, the hand is for loving, not martial arts. The hand on a diapered bottom is useless as a spanking, but effective in causing permanent damage to the spine. There is no surface pain to the child thus whipped. Any pain would be deep inside, similar to a fall or a car wreck. Any spanking, to effectively reinforce instruction, must cause pain. It is most effective to strike the rod against bare skin, where nerves are located at the surface. A surface sting will cause sufficient pain, with no injury or bruising. Select your instrument according to the child's size. For the under one year old, a small, ten- to twelve-inch long, willowy branch (stripped of any knots that might break the skin), about one-eighth inch in diameter is sufficient. Sometimes alternatives have to be sought. A one-foot ruler, or its equivalent in a paddle, is a sufficient alternative. For the larger child, a belt or larger tree branch is effective.

A CAUTION TO RECIPIENTS OF THE MILLSTONE AWARD

There are always some that act in the extreme. These individuals could use what has been said about the legitimate use of the rod to justify ongoing brutality to their children. I can think of several right now. These abusers of their children would not in the least view themselves as such. They would call themselves "strong disciplinarians." *"But whoso shall offend one of these little ones which believe in me, it were better for him that a millstone were hanged about his neck and that he were drowned in the depth of the sea (Matt. 18:6)."*

FORMS OF ABUSE

Only a few parents are categorically abusive. But many parents sometimes give in to anger and employ abusive methods. The child is rebellious. The parent suddenly loses it and screams out. Like a whirlwind, he snatches the child up by the arm and gives him several bangs on the bottom. The father's eyes burn, his brow hardens. His pulse rate soars. Anger is the best word to describe his feelings. Smash! Subdue! "You will do what I say. You are not going to do this to me little girl!" Red faced, muscles tensed. Anyone looking at the face of a parent in this state would think there was a war in progress.

The rod should not be a vent for parents' anger. In the daily course of life, many people experience anger and feel the need to strike out. There is no place for this selfish, vindictive streak in the discipline of children. Where the supreme motivation is anything other than the child's good, there will be problems.

I am ashamed to say that in most cases the rod is administered at the end of an intolerance curve. Average parents are quite predictable in their "discipline." They go through a warm-up exercise of threats that increase their irritation until their anger generates a will to retaliate against the child. What follows is a riot, not Biblical chastisement.

There is a political move to outlaw spanking. They say, "If you hit a child, he will grow up to be violent." The people who advocate rodless training do not believe the Bible. They judge others by their own experience. The only time they have "hit" their child, or been tempted to, is when they were angry. They are correct in saying that what they call "hitting" the child may cause him to grow up and use violence as a way of resolving conflicts. But they do not understand the Christian heart. Having never experienced it, they cannot fathom the self-restraint and love that motivates true Christians. The problem is that spanking is practiced by many people motivated by self-interest, and this is what the spanking abolitionists are seeing and experiencing.

COMMON SCENARIO

"Johnny, stop climbing on that stool. You could break something. Did you hear what I said? I am not going to tell you again. What do you mean, 'No?' Now you do what I tell you to—right now. DO YOU HEAR ME?!! GEEETT DOWNNN!!! I have had about all I am going to take from you. Why are you always so hard headed? You are driving me crazy! This is absolutely the last time I am going to tell you... GET DOWN!!!" Then she tells him several more times. At this point it is a competition between the emotionally disturbed mother and the little boy. A cauldron of anger and resentment has built up in this mother that is momentarily at a near killing rage. It is this exact feeling that, in greater proportions and in the less restrained, leads to murder dozens of times every day. Her hostility gushes forth. Like a striking snake, her arm becomes a bungie cord, yanking the child from the stool, swinging him screaming through the air. With the other bare hand she strikes out at his bottom in a wild spray of flat-handed, karate chops. The gyrating child, his little shoulder nearly dislocated, screams his protest and defiance. The mother has vented her anger and is ready to resume her routine. The child goes off to plot his next escapade. This has no more resemblance to discipline than a playground fight.

Once the parent's feelings of personal injury are expelled through this act of violence (that's what it is in the case described) and the kid flees from sight, or appears sufficiently subdued not to cause the parent more trouble, the parent is satisfied. "Forget the kid. He will not cause ME any more trouble for awhile."

A truly concerned parent is going to patiently instruct the child for his own good. The rod must be accompanied by reproof in order to give wisdom. By reproof, we don't mean ranting and raving. You reprove a child by teaching him the principles involved in the conduct you demand. You explain why his behavior is unacceptable and offer suggestions on how he should conduct himself.

Parents who know that they lack self-control often swing the pendulum to the extreme and cease to use the rod when the child really needs it. Their own life is so out of control and filled with guilt that they recognize their inability to be objective and fair in discipline. Their unwillingness to repent and bring their own life into balance will cause the children to suffer from lack of proper administration of the rod.

One of the marks of the unbalanced use of the rod is the lack of accompanying instruction. *"The rod and reproof give wisdom (Prov. 29:15)."* Where there is just a venting of the parent's anger, there will be no careful, patient, concerned reproof. The rod should be viewed as an aid to instruction in that it reinforces reproof. It should never be the last resort, forced on us by our frustration. Reproof without the rod is equally unbalanced, for it leaves the impression that the law has no teeth.

CHAPTER 7
Philosophy of the Rod

THE TEACHING ROD

For a little while God has placed the soul of your child under your tutelage. Your home is a moral workshop where you help God prepare your child for heavenly citizenship. The developing child benefits from growing up in a home that mimics the government of God. Proper application of the rod is essential in causing the child to understand the judgment of God—and eventually the grace of God.

In the limited world of the child, parents are representatives of truth and justice, dispensers of punishment and reward. A child's parents are the window through which he develops a view of what God is like and how moral government functions. If you make rules and do not respect them enough to enforce them, you will be making a statement about law in general. Your responses to transgressions are stage-playing the responses of God. By proper application of the rod they will come to understand the concept of law and accountability. Unless all transgression, rebellion, and meanness of spirit are treated as God treats sin, the child's world-view will be false. If temporal authorities do not honor the law enough to enforce it with punishment, why should the child expect the great, eternal authority to be any different?

The military uses real bullets in training men to avoid enemy fire. Replacing the rod with hollow threats would be to your children like replacing live bullets with blanks. It would get the men killed later in real battle.

THE FEAR OF GOD

A child must take seriously the moral law. *"The fear of the LORD is the beginning of wisdom (Prov. 9:10)."* In defining the root of sin, Paul said, *"There is no fear of God before their eyes (Rom. 3:18)."* The proper use of the rod teaches a wholesome fear. Do not fall victim to the modern rewriting of *"fear"* as "respect." For Jesus said, *"But I will forewarn you whom ye shall fear: Fear him, which after he hath killed hath power to cast into hell; yea, I say unto you, Fear him (Luke 12:5)."* The Scripture makes a distinction between honor, love, and fear: *"Honour all men. Love the brotherhood. Fear God. Honour the king (1Pet. 2:17)."*

Though we don't have *"the spirit of fear,"* we who understand eternity fear to be in opposition to the *"Avenger"* of all evil. Remember, you are preparing your child for real living in a real world and to face a real God in a real judgment of real accountability to a reward in a real eternity. This is no game; the rewards are great, the loss too horrible for a parent not to make this top priority. Use of the rod is not optional with a Bible believer. It is God's design for proper training. The souls of your children are at stake.

UNDERSTANDING GRACE

The end a Christian has in view is not just submission to the rule of law, but that the child should understand the grace of God. Only through the naked sword of the law are we pressed into an understanding of grace. The law is *"our schoolmaster to bring us unto Christ (Gal. 3:24)."* God could not show Himself on Mount Calvary until He first showed Himself on Mount Sinai.

By strictly enforcing the rules of the household through legislation, accountability, and punishment, you not only teach your children to fear and respect the Lawgiver, but you create opportunities to demonstrate grace. What a sacred and wonderful responsibility!

CHAPTER 8
Selective Subjection

I DON'T HAVE TO OBEY YOU

Some children have a very irritating habit—selective subjection. Have you ever tried to correct a child, only to be impudently told, "You are not my mother, you can't tell me what to do?" (Most likely, the mother can't tell him what to do either.) That response tells you that even when the child is obedient to his parents, down inside he is totally rebellious. He is not under any authority other than his own.

If the child perceived some devious intent on the part of the adult and was resisting abduction or something akin to it, such boldness would be in order. But don't delude yourself into being proud of your child's actions as if it was loyalty or caution. It is rebellion, which is as the *"sin of witchcraft (1 Sam 15:23)."* Even when rebuked by another child, a properly trained child will see the rule of law behind the rebuke and come under subjection.

There is by nature in every child an innate awareness of his duty to conform to the common law of love and benevolence. This unwritten code is expressed when one small child says to another, "You ought not do that." The conscience that is not yet seared is constantly appealing for conformity to this innate standard. When a child rebels against the just rebukes of his peers, he is not only rebelling against his peers, but against the "rule of law" in general. The child need not be conscious of this "rule of law." Most adults aren't, but it shadows everyone. For example, a child may not know what the word "rebellion" means, yet function exactly as an adult functions when in a state of rebellion. The child is violating his own conscience. He is suffering guilt. He is building a barrier of pride, self-love, and will become self-loathing. A child encouraged or permitted to thus continue is destined to moral destruction.

THE OLDER SISTER

My two youngest daughters, when nine and eleven years old, were entertaining some children we were keeping. A two-year-old girl picked up an item that was off limits. Her older sister, fourteen, told her she couldn't play with it and proceeded to take it away. The child threw a screaming fit. (That was her normal approach in paying back her parents. They considered her behavior normal.)

My nine-year-old, amazed at this bizarre behavior, came and told her mother. Upon investigating, Deb found the little girl was mad at her big sister. The younger girl felt that her older sister should have no jurisdiction over her behavior. The fourteen-year-old admitted she was not allowed to discipline her little sister. My wife immediately set up a training session. She took the forbidden object and placed it back on the floor in front of the child. You may say, "But that is tempting the child!" Did not God do the same for Adam and Eve?

The child immediately stopped crying, in triumph looked at her sister, and reached for the object. Deb said, "No, you can't have that." When the child grabbed it anyway, Deb, saying "No," spatted her hand with a little switch. She left the object within inches of the child's grasp. Since the object was not out of reach, the child assumed it was still within limits. When she again reached, Deb gave her a spat and a calm command. After one or two more times, the child learned her lesson.

Deb then handed the object to the older sister and told her to place it in front of the child and tell her "No." As the fourteen-year-old extended the object to the child, she reached out, only to jerk her hand back when told "No." The forbidden object was then left on the floor in the middle of the playroom. The little girl played around it the rest of the day without touching it. The little girl who had previously made everyone miserable by her demands was cheerful and congenial until time to leave.

KEEPING REBELLION ALIVE

To allow your child a time of rebellion and self-will (whether it is around your spouse, grandparents, older brothers or sisters, the baby sitter, or peers) is to allow rebellion and self-will to stay alive. The seeds of rebellion will always be there to come to fruition when the external pressures are lessened. You may be controlling their outward actions, but you are not building character.

In a family submitted to the light of God, children will be so surrendered to the unspoken principle of conduct that they readily give and receive rebuke from one another. In the church, we are all accountable to one another. It should be so in the home.y

Furthermore, the older children will be more responsible when given responsibility over the younger children. And what a load it takes off the mother! Though older children are placed in charge of the younger ones, the younger children are always allowed a court of appeal. If the older child abuses his or her authority, you should treat it as a grave offense. The younger children soon learn that to make an unfounded claim against the older child's discipline is to receive double discipline. The responsibility given to the older child is valuable training. It also lessens tensions, since the older child is not left helpless in the presence of an unrestrained little brother or sister. In a home where only parents enforce obedience, siblings will never like each other, and older children will despise their little brothers and sisters. When two kids are together, one should be in charge.

BLESSED MOTHER, HAVE MERCY

A number of times I have observed the difficult situation where one parent (usually the less sentimental father) is firm in training for obedience, but the other parent (usually the mother) gives in to sympathy and is slack to demand instant obedience. During the day while the father is away, the mother begs, nags, threatens, and after a while, becomes sufficiently angry to impress upon the children the need to yield temporary compliance.

The father comes home from work and is soon confronted with the rebellion and disobedience of his children. When he spanks the children, they wail cries of injustice. The emotionally weak mother so suffers from seeing her babies "abused" by this "stranger" invading their domain that, in front of the children, she steps in to challenge his judgments. The children soon learn how to play the mother's emotions against the father's "justice." As the mother becomes more and more critical of the father and protective of the children, the children become liars and learn to manipulate the contentious adults.

The father sees that he is losing control and bears down harder on the children. The mother, attempting to provide a balance, becomes even slacker, and the gulf between them widens. The children suffer.

One parent should NEVER correct or question the other's judgment in the presence of the children. It is better for your child if you support an occasional injustice than to destroy the authority base by your open division. We see this manifested when a child that is being disciplined by the father begins to plead for his mother. When a child runs to the mother, the mother should take up the discipline as forcefully as the father would. If a father is attempting to make a child eat his oats and the child cries for his mother, then the mother should respond by spanking the child for whining for her **and** for not eating his oats. He will then be glad to be dealing only with the father.

We broke this tendency to selective subjection early. When one of us was spanking one of our children and they cried for the other, the other parent would come over and contribute to the spanking. After two or three times of that, the child decided that one parent was enough.

After a child has been spanked, he should not be allowed to flee to the other parent for sympathy. It is important that he find his solace in the one who did the spanking. When God chastens us, it is to draw us to Himself, not to cause us to turn to another.

Mother, if you think your husband is too forceful in his discipline, there is something you can do. While he is away, demand, expect, train for, and discipline to receive instant and complete obedience from your children. When Father comes home, the house will be peaceful and well ordered. The children will always obey their father, giving him no need to discipline them.

CHAPTER 9
Training Examples

STRIKING OUT

As my wife was counseling with a young mother, I watched a most amazing scene unfold. A two-year-old boy, upon failing to get his mother's attention, picked up a plastic toy wrench and began to pound his mother's arm. Occasionally he would reach up and poke her in the face. This was not new behavior. We had previously observed him follow in the footsteps of Cain as he perpetrated acts of violence on his little brother. On a previous day my wife observed him slamming a tricycle wheel down on his mother's foot. She would cry out, "Johnny (The name has been changed to protect the guilty mother), that hurts Mother." And, in a whining voice, "Don't hurt your Mother." Wham!! Down goes the tricycle wheel on her foot again. "Stop it, that hurts!" I'll tell you what hurts. It hurts to see a mother abuse her child by doing nothing while her responses are making a criminal out of little Johnny.

Well, on this occasion it would turn out differently. As the talk continued, little Johnny got tired of assaulting his mother and turned on my wife. She was not his mother and was not trained to take his abuse, so without looking at him, and while the conversation continued unabated, Deb picked up a matching toy wrench and held it casually. She was preparing to teach the mother and the son a lesson. When little Johnny struck my wife again, without interrupting the conversation, and showing no anger or agitation, she returned the blow with more than matching force. Such surprise! What is this little Johnny feels coming from his arm? Pain! And somehow it is associated with the striking of this toy. Again, Johnny strikes. Again, swift reprisal (training really). Johnny is very tough; so, though he didn't cry, he pulled back his pained arm and examined it carefully. You could see the little mental computer working. As if to test his new theory, again, but with less force, he struck. The immediately returned blow was not diminished in strength. This time, I thought he would cry. No, after looking at his mother as if to say, "What is this new thing?" he again and with even less force struck my wife on the arm. I was thinking, "She will lighten up this time and match his diminished intensity." Again, as if disinterested, my wife forcefully returned the blow.

Now you may wonder what the mother was doing during this time. Believe it or not, the two women continued to talk, my wife, as if all was normal, the mother, with a facial expression divided between wonder and mild alarm. Johnny, tough enough for Special Forces, did one of those pained, crying faces, covered by a forced smile. To my amazement, with one-fourth the original force, he again struck my wife. Again, she returned the blow. I was hoping that Johnny was getting close to learning his lesson. The conversation had about died in anticipation of the outcome. Johnny must have had a Viking lineage, for he continued to trade blows about ten times. On Johnny's part, the blows got lighter and lighter until after a short, contemplative delay, he gave a little tap that was returned with a swift, forceful blow. He let the toy wrench lay limp in his hand while he studied my wife's face. I think he was puzzled by her relaxed, non-threatening expression. He was accustomed to being argued with and threatened. He had been trained to expect building antagonism to precede confrontation. My wife never even spoke to him, hardly looked at him, and gave a friendly smile when she did.

Well, Johnny was a lot smarter than the cat that learned to keep his tail out from under the rocker. He turned away from my wife, shrugged his shoulders, bounced his legs, smiled, examined his arm and looked at the wrench still in his hand. I could see an idea come into his experimental little head. He turned to his mother and pounded her on the arm. As she rubbed her arm and cried, "Johnneeeee, that hurrrrrt!" my wife handed her another toy wrench. The next time Johnny struck, the young mother courageously returned the blow. It only took two or three times to learn his lesson for good. The mother was also being taught. If she remained consistent, Johnny would be forever broken of his tendency to be a bully.

Please understand that <u>the mother's use of the toy wrench was not a substitute for the rod</u>. This was not discipline, but training. The child was cheerfully striking with the toy. Though frustrated, he was not angry or mean. Had that been the case, his medicine would have been the rod. The returned blows were teaching him that what he was doing was painful and undesirable. He was also being taught that there were others who could give it out better than he. Meeting a bigger bully cures most little bullies. Children learn not to pick up wasps by picking up one.

Most people would find it hard to believe that this encounter endeared my wife to little Johnny. He seems to love her dearly and demands to be picked up when she is near. Children are comfortable around someone that has control of their own emotions and with whom they know their limitations. Since this experience and further counseling, the mother and the child are showing great improvement.

LITTLE FOXES SPOIL THE VINES

We just returned from having supper with some good neighbors. They are a fine young couple who are just beginning their family. They are kind parents, concerned to rear their children properly. They would never be guilty of abuse or neglect. Their children are their priority. But, as we sat talking, I was once again reminded that it is the little "insignificant" things that determine a child's character.

Their little three-year-old boy was between us, playing with a small, rubber, bathtub goat. He apparently discovered there was still some water in it, so he held it over the table and began to squeeze. To the delight of everyone, and especially the boy, the goat began to relieve itself on the table. After a good laugh, the mother went to the kitchen for a towel.

When she attempted to wipe the table, the little fellow said "No" and tried to prevent her from removing his water puddle. She easily brushed him aside and wiped the puddle away. He gasped an angry and frustrated protest, threw himself onto the couch, and cried. The cry was not loud and did not last five seconds before he jerked around with protruded lip to see what other entertainment was available. It was all over in ten seconds.

The conversation resumed as he performed the first of a series of deliberate transgressions. He climbed onto the coffee table—which is always off limits—and then sought out other expressions of defiance. After about the fifth command, he would cease and go to the next transgression. The conversation continued with only an occasional lapse while he was being rebuked. This is exactly the kind of issue that demands concentrated training and discipline. To ignore it as they did is to waste your child.

What did the child learn? He learned that his mother is bigger than he is and can force her will upon him. This will result in his enforcing his will upon his younger brother. He learned that he does not have to exercise self-control. Anything that he is big enough to achieve is fair game. The anger that was allowed to seethe in his heart led to rebellion. Though the parents were unaware of it, his subsequent actions were the product of his defiled heart.

THE PROPER RESPONSE

The proper response would have gone something like this: "Johnny, here is a rag. Please clean up your mess." "No, I don't wanna." He then continues to dabble in the water, sort of rocking back and forth with one shoulder and with his chin down, not too earnestly involved in the water, yet waiting to see if his mother is going to let him be. Rebellion is in his heart, but he faces a superior power, so he hesitates. Again she says, "Johnny, clean the water up now." (With my children, one command is all they would get.) If he again hesitates, she goes for the switch. If he hurriedly attempts to avert a switching by cleaning the water, it makes no difference. She returns with the switch, and standing in front of him, says, "Johnny I told you to wipe up the water, and you hesitated. Therefore I am going to have to spank you so you will not hesitate the next time. Mama wants her boy to grow up to be wise like Daddy, so I am going to help you to remember to obey. Lean over the couch. Put your hands down. Now, don't move or I will have to give you more licks."

She then administers about ten slow, patient licks on his bare legs. He cries in pain. If he continues to show defiance by jerking around and defending himself, or by expressing anger, then she will wait a moment and again lecture him and again spank him. When it is obvious that he is totally broken, she will hand him the rag and very calmly say, "Johnny, clean up your mess." He should very contritely wipe up the water. To test and reinforce this moment of surrender, give him another command. "Johnny, go over and put all of your toys back in the box." Or, "Johnny, pick up all the dirty clothes and put them in the basket." After three or four faithfully performed acts of obedience, brag on how "smart" a helper he is. For the rest of the day, he will be happy and compliant. The transformation is unbelievable.

You have just witnessed the potential making of a peaceful home and of an emotionally stable and obedient child. If you are faithful to guard against and reward every infraction, whether in attitude or action, in just a few days you will have a perfectly obedient and cheerful child.

I DON'T HAVE THE TIME

Now, I know exactly what some of you are thinking. "But, I am pushed to the limit now. I don't have the time to watch and guard against every transgression." <u>If you have duties outside the home that prevent you from properly rearing your children, give your duties back to the Devil.</u> I mean that, even if they are church activities. If you have children, your first calling is that of a parent. If, on the other hand, you are over-extended because of a chaotic household, then you cannot afford to do other than be faithful in discipline, for you need the rest it will bring.

Just yesterday, a young mother of small children came to the house and told my wife this story: "This morning, as I was sitting at the sewing machine, my four-year-old son came to me and said, 'Mother, I love you so much.' I stopped sewing, looked at the earnest expression on his face, and said, 'I'm glad you love me, for I love you too. You are such a fine boy.' As I attempted to turn back to sewing, he said, 'Do you know why I love you so much?' 'No, why do you love me so?' 'Because, you make me bring in firewood and do what you say.'"

This mother always looks fresh and rested. I know this sounds pretentious, but it is the absolute truth. Even a four-year-old can compare himself with other children and appreciate his parents' guidance.

A SWITCH AT NAP TIME SAVES MINE

When your baby is tired and sleepy enough to become irritable, don't reinforce his irritability by allowing the cause to continue. Put the little one to sleep. But what of the grouch who would rather complain than sleep? Get tough. Be firm with him. Never put him down and then for some reason reverse your position, allowing him to get up. For your reputation with the child, you must follow through. He may not be able to sleep, but he can be trained to lie there quietly. He will very quickly come to know that any time he is laid down there is no alternative but to stay put. To get up is to be on the firing line and get switched back down. It will become as easy as putting a rag doll to bed. Those who are MOSTLY consistent must use the switch more often. Those who are ALWAYS consistent will come to never need it.

When you first begin to train your child to lie down quietly, he may whimper and protest, which is just a natural expression of disappointment. If you ignore whimpering, it will pass. But if you reward the whimpering by letting him get up, he will repeat it the next time he wants to get up. Having discovered the power of whimpering, he will continue to employ it to get his way. By allowing the child to dictate policy, you are training him to be a "brat." Since this whining and crying is eventually going to annoy Mother, it is better, regardless of the mother's feelings, to break this tendency before it takes root and becomes a personality habit. It is sickening to see teenagers whine.

Just think of it, children who never beg, whine, or cry for anything! We have raised five whineless children. Think of the convenience of being able to lay your children down and say, "Nap time," and then lie down yourself, knowing that they will all be lying quietly in bed when you awake.

OBEDIENCE

As one mother was reading an early manuscript of this book, she became aware of her twelve-month-old daughter whining and pulling on her. When she came to the part above, about not allowing a child to whine ("If they are tired put them to bed."), she decided to apply what she was reading. She put her daughter down and told her to go to sleep. The sleepy child responded by crying in protest. Following the book's instructions, she spanked the child and told her to stop crying and go to sleep. The child had previously been trained to spend an hour intermittently crying and getting up, only to be fussed at and laid back down. Nevertheless, the spanking subdued the crying and caused her to lie still. The mother continued her reading. After a while she looked up to see that the child had very quietly slipped to the floor to browse through a book. The mother smiled at how sweet and quiet the child was and continued reading the manuscript.

Reading further, she contemplated the fact that the child had not obeyed. "But she is being so good and is not bothering me," the mother thought. She then realized the issue was not whether the child was bothering her, but whether or not she was learning to obey. She rightly concluded that by allowing the child to quietly sit on the floor at the foot of her bed, where she would eventually go to sleep, she was effectively training the child to be in rebellion to the rule of law. Out of love for her child, this mother inconvenienced herself and shattered the quiet solitude by spanking the child and again telling her to stay in the bed and go to sleep. The child went to sleep immediately.

THREE-YEAR-OLD MOTHER

The other day at our house, a three-year-old little girl was playing with dolls. (Let me interject: All children's dolls should be BABY dolls, not "Barbie" dolls. The fantasy arising from playing with baby dolls causes the child to role-play mother. The fantasy arising from Barbie dolls causes a child to role-play a sex goddess. *"As a* [child] *thinketh in his heart so is he (Prov. 23:7).")* This little girl was role-playing mother. The thing that was interesting was the role this little "mother" assumed with her baby. In her imagination the baby started crying after being given a command. She scolded her baby and then turned her over and spanked her. Then she spoke comforting, reassuring words and praised her baby for being good. She perfectly mimicked the loving, patient tone and firmness of her own mother.

As I continued to peek in at the proceedings, she continued her "mother practice" session. Several situations arose with her rag baby, which she promptly and firmly dealt with like an old pro. In fact, I could not have handled the make-believe situations any better. She told the screaming child (the rag doll) "No! That's not nice. You can't have it now. Stop your crying. SWITCH, SWITCH. If you don't stop crying, mama will have to spank you again. SWITCH, SWITCH, SWITCH. OK, stop crying now. That's better. Now see if you can play happily."

Here was a three-year-old "mother" already prepared to train up happy and obedient children. She knew exactly what to expect from her mother. And what was even more amazing, she knew exactly what her mother expected from her. She disciplined her baby doll for atti-tudes, not actions. This little, three-year-old girl was completely trained. The battle was won. As long as her parents consistently maintain what they have already instilled, she will never be anything but a blessing.

BEGGARS CAN'T BE CHOOSERS

A child should NEVER whine or beg. This is an easy habit to break. Never reward a beggar, and the begging will go away. In our house, the one sure way of not getting your desire was to beg or whine. We went out of our way to not reward a begging child. If we had pur-chased a treat for the children, and one of them became impatient and whined for it or asked twice, he was certain to be excluded, even if it meant that he was left to watch the other children eat the treat for which he had begged. If I was preparing to pick up a small child and he whined to be picked up, then I did not pick him up until he became distracted and pleasant—even though it meant inconvenience for me.

You may envision such a rule being enforced in your house to the tune of constant wailings of injustice. The very thought of it may make you feel like a tyrant. If you gave it a try, being 99% consistent, you would not be satisfied with the results. If a child ever gets his way through begging or whining, he will try it ten times until it works again. If his experience of begging proves to be counterproductive, he will soon stop wasting his energy in fruitless whining. <u>When beggars can't choose, they choose not to beg</u>.

THE HARD WAY

For two years after the birth of our first child, my wife was unable to conceive. When she finally did, she had a miscarriage. Then, one year later, the little fellow whose name we had picked out five years earlier was finally born. Our first son! My wife was ever so possessive. By the age of one, he was so attached to her that I had to submit a request well in advance if I wanted to spend some time with her alone. He could not be left with a baby sitter unless she was blessed with deafness. I didn't know much about children then, and thought this was just a stage that would run its course. A friend who had more experience as a father was the one to show me otherwise.

I guess the men of the church had all they could take of this two-year-old with the umbilical cord still attached. My wife was the child's willing slave until that fateful day in April. I can still see my friend walking up to the car where we were unloading at a church outing. With the other conspirators shadowed in the background, he came up to my wife, reached out, swept Gabriel away, and said, "I'll take him," and was gone.

I couldn't understand what he wanted with that bucking, screaming, desperate kid, who was reaching back over his shoulder pleading with his mother to rescue him. His accomplices closed in behind him as if to prevent any rescue. I supposed the misguided fellows would soon want to return him like one would want to return a cold to its donor.

To my wife it was the opposite of giving birth. She was being weaned. After a couple of hours, the "trainers" came back around with a new Gabriel, laughing and enjoying the men's company. He didn't run to his mother or resume his crying.

To our amazement, from that moment on the umbilical cord was dried up, and we had a little boy whose world was larger than his mother's arms. Ha! And I had my wife back! The next boy was soon on the way, but he did not come to be an extension of his mother's self-image.

AS THE WHEEL TURNS

When we baby-sit for other people, it is always on the condition that we have full liberty to discipline and train. We try to be realistic and use discretion in determining what can be effectively accomplished in the time allotted. We consider the child's trust in us, his or her acquaintance with our technique, the parents' sensitivity, and the child's emotional state.

On one occasion, Deb was keeping a mixed group of about ten children and babies, all from four different families attending a seminar. One couple's first child, about fifteen months old, was highly overindulged and showed it. He had been trained to expect constant catering and pacifying. He was missing his "mother-servant," and was complaining. It was not just the "I'm sad and lonesome, won't someone love me?" His crying said, "I'm mad as all get out. Things are not going my way. Where is my mama anyway? I'm going to make everyone pay for this treatment. This will be a night they will not want to repeat. I'll see to it."

The children were all placed at the table for a snack. After a couple of minutes, the little fellow began to pout. He didn't like the food or the company. He got down and began to complain. Giving him more leeway than we would have one of our own, my wife handed him a potato chip, for which he had previously shown delight. True to his attitude, he defiantly threw it on the floor.

My ever patient wife, who was also quite busy, picked him up and placed him in a big, soft chair, handing him a brightly colored roller-skate. She took a moment to show him what fun it was to hold it upside down and turn the wheels. "See, turn the wheels," she said. With defiance, he turned his face away. This otherwise sweet child had developed (rather the parents had developed) a selfish and rebellious spirit. If left to himself, he will *"bring his mother to shame."* My wife always had a special fondness for this child, and it hurt her to see him developing such a nasty attitude.

She decided it was showdown time. She ignored the other children, who were happily investigating and rearranging everything on the table, and quickly obtained her switch (twelve inches long and about the diameter of a small noodle). She again placed the skate in front of him and gently and playfully said, "Turn the wheels." Again, he defiantly turned his head away whimpering. She again demonstrated the fun of rolling the wheels and repeated the command. Again, defiance.

This time, being assured he fully understood it to be a command, she placed his hand on the wheels, repeated the command, and when no obedience followed, she switched his leg. Again, in a mild but firm voice she commanded him to turn the wheels. Self-will dies hard. My wife brought other children over to demonstrate the fun of wheel turning. Pulling his hand as far from the skate as possible, he covered his right hand with his left—apparently to reinforce his resolve, or to demonstrate it—and refused to turn the wheels.

After about ten acts of stubborn defiance, followed by ten switchings, he surrendered his will to one higher than himself. In rolling the wheels, he did what every accountable human being must do—he humbled himself before the highest authority and admitted that his interests are not paramount. After one begrudged roll, my wife turned to other chores.

A few minutes later she noticed he was turning the wheels and laughing with the other children—with whom he had previously shown only disdain. The surly attitude was all gone. In its place was contentment, thankfulness, and a fellowship with his peers. The "rod" had lived up to its Biblical promise.

CHAPTER 10
Safety Training

Some training has nothing to do with character building. It just keeps your child alive and healthy. These illustrations may sound harsh to some, but I have proven, along with many others, that this approach is both effective and safe.

GUN SAFETY

Being a hunting family, we have always had guns around the house. With our little ones, we made sure to keep the guns out of reach. But with the possibility of them sooner or later coming in contact with a loaded gun, we trained them for safety.

With our first toddler, I placed an old, unused and empty, single-shot shotgun in the living room corner. After taking the toddlers through several No-saying, hand-switching sessions, they knew guns were always off limits. Every day they played around the gun without touching it. I never had to be concerned with their going into someone else's house and touching a gun. I didn't gun-proof my house, I gun-proofed my children.

HOT STOVE

We've always had a wood burning stove for cooking and heating. A red-hot stove can seriously burn toddlers. I have seen some awful scars. But we had no fear, knowing the effectiveness of training. When the first fires of fall were lit, I would coax the toddlers over to see the fascinating flames. Of course, they always wanted to touch, so I held them off until the stove got hot enough to inflict pain without deep burning—testing it with my own hand. When the heat was just right, I would open the door long enough for them to be attracted by the flames, and then I would move away. The child would inevitably run to the stove and touch it. Just as his hand touched the stove, I would say, "Hot!" It usually took two, sometimes three times, but they all learned their lessons. Other than the training session, where we never raised a blister, we never had a child get burned. It was so effective that, thereafter, if I wanted to see them do a back flip, all I had to do was say, "Hot!!" They would even turn loose of a glass of iced tea.

SINKING FEELING

When our children were young, we had a pond in the immediate yard. As they grew to be toddlers, wandering around outside, we always watched them closely. Yet, knowing the possibility of one getting out of sight, we cranked up the training. On a warm spring day I followed the first set of wobbly legs to the inviting water. She played around the edge until she found a way to get down the bank to the water. I stood close by as she bent over, reaching into the mirror of shining color. Splash! In she went. I restrained my anxiety long enough for her to right herself in the cold water and show some recognition of her inability to breathe. When panic set in (mine as well as hers—not to mention her mother's), I pulled her out and scolded her for getting close to the pond. She didn't swallow any water, and there was no need for resuscitation—except on my wife, who took several hours to begin breathing normally. We repeated the same process with all the children. It only took one time for each of them to learn respect for the water. And it sure made life easier for us.

We did have trouble with one of them. She is the one that became mobile early, crawling at four months and walking at seven. She always had marvelous coordination. She just wouldn't fall in. I got weary taking walks to the pond. So to bring the class to graduation, I pushed. Oh, she didn't know it. As she was balanced over the water, I just nudged her with my foot. To this day I still believe that if I had left her alone she would have been able to swim out. But, it distressed her enough to make her not want to play around the pond.

No, they didn't stay fearful of the water. My children were all swimming by the time they were four. We still watched them closely, and we never had a close call. The training worked. Do not try this unless you are sure that you can maintain full control of all the circumstances.

GET OUT FAST

One winter, when my two girls were nine and eleven, they were riding with me in an old 4x4 Army truck. The gravel road was bumpy and rough. When I made a stop at an intersection, I heard the two, 12-volt batteries, located right behind the seats, short out and begin to arc.

An explosion of spraying battery acid was potentially imminent. The girls understood none of this. However, when I commanded (this time in a raised voice), "Get out fast!" they didn't ask, "Why?" I immediately got out on my side to run around and open their usually jammed door. As soon as I cleared the door on my side, I looked over my shoulder to see how they were doing. They were gone. The door was still closed, and the window, which also sticks, was only open about half way. But they were nowhere in sight. When I got around to the other side, there they were, piled up in the gravel road rubbing sore hands and knees. "How did you get out?" I asked. "Through the window," they choked out. "Head first?" I asked. "You said get out fast," was their accusing reply.

My son, who was driving another truck behind me, said, "I didn't know what was happening. Suddenly they both came flying out the window head first and landed in the road." I had trained them to jump upon command. They did. There may come a time when their safety or survival will depend on instant obedience. "Duck!" or "Hit the deck!" has saved more than one life.

TRAIN FOR REALITY

The world is sometimes a hostile place. A child must learn to take precautions early. Don't give your child a modified sense of reality. Teach them about heights and falling, about guns, the danger of knives and scissors, the caution of sharp sticks and coat-hanger wires, the terror of fire, and the danger of poisons and electricity. School them. Drill them. Show them examples. Expose them to death—the death of a pet or an accident victim. This must be done with calm, confident reverence, not with fear. Don't be excessive. One or two examples to a three-year-old are enough. Control their environment, but don't shut out reality. Expose them to it at a level they can comprehend and at a rate suitable to their maturity. The goal is to keep the training ahead of any external assaults and to have them worldly wise by the time they must face it on their own.

SNAP TO IT!

I am the General. My wife is my aid and adviser—the first in-command when I am absent. I rule benevolently. Love and respect are my primary tools of persuasion. I lead, not command from a distant bunker. Mine know that I will lay down my life for them; consequently, they will lay down theirs for me. They find joy and pride in being part of the team. To instantly obey a command is their part of the team-work. In doing so, the home team runs smoothly and our common objectives are met.

I have taught the children to obey first and ask questions later. When they were small and I put them through paces, they learned to immediately do what I said. If they ever failed to instantly obey a command, I would "drill" them. "Sit down. Don't speak until I tell you to." Understand, I was not taking out frustrations. It was all done with utmost pleasantness. "Stand up," I would say. "Now come here. Go touch the door." And, before they could get there, "Sit." Plop, down they would go. "Now, go to your rooms and clean them up." Just like little, proud soldiers, off they would go to the task.

If one of them should fail in his attitude, he would be spanked—without haste or hostility, mind you. Negligence or clumsi-ness was a time for patience and grace, but lazy rebellion was punished with the rod.

This may sound cold and harsh. I hope it doesn't, for it was warm, friendly, loving, and produced confident, calm, hard working, loyal children and adults. In actuality, because of our consistency, the children were seldom spanked. They soon learned that every transgres-sion received a *"just recompense of reward."* They knew that without a doubt, delayed obedience meant a meeting with the rod. Delayed obe-dience was dealt with as disobedience. Such firmness with consistency gives the children security.

Even today, without looking at the children, I can snap my finger, pointing to the floor, and they all (including the ones over six-feet) immediately sit. I can point to the door, and they all exit. When a visit develops into a counseling session, I have given the gesture for the children to vacate the room, and the company never knew what prompted everyone to leave. Teach your children to "snap to it." They will be better for it, and it will make them more lovable—which makes for more loving.

CHAPTER 11
Potty Untraining

NO MORE DIAPERS

On a missionary trip to Central America, we were amazed by the practice of the primitive Maya Indians in not diapering their babies prior to stuffing them into a carrying pouch. Their infants were all potty trained. After experimenting on our own, and after further observation, we discovered that infants are born with an aversion to going in their "nests." Parents "untrain" them by forcing them to become accustomed to going in their clothes. A child instinctively protests a bowel movement. He kicks, stiffens, and complains. Being sensitive to the warning signs (after having changed 17,316 diapers with the first three), my wife tried it on our new arrivals. When she sensed that the child was about to "go," she would go to the toilet and place the bare infant against her bare legs in a spread-leg sitting position. Dribbling a little stream of warm water over the child's private parts helped provoke the start of an impending "tinkle." As the child began urinating, she would say, "Pee Pee." On other occasions, if she missed the signs and a bowel movement was in progress, she would rush the child to the bathroom to finish on the toilet, while occasionally saying, "Do Do." Even if the child was through with his elimination, she still set him on the pot in order to reinforce the training. He came to identify the sound with the muscle function. Our children became so well trained to the voice command that we had to be careful not to say the words at the wrong time. We could be bragging to our neighbor, say the magic words, and induce a release.

Now, some disbelieving mothers have said, "You are the one who is potty trained, not the baby." Just as a mother knows her baby is hungry or sleepy, she can tell if he wants to go potty. A three-week-old baby is doing all he can to communicate.

My mother-in-law was equally skeptical until the day my wife said to her, "Stop at the next station, the baby wants to go potty." They stopped, and as Deb came out with a thoroughly relieved three-month-old, my mother-in-law was convinced.

For a while, our bathroom became the end of a pilgrimage for those seeking faith in infant potty training. Many a time our red faced, infant girls looked up to see a great cloud of amazed witnesses expectantly hovering in our large bathroom.

Understand, the child is not made to sit for long periods of time waiting to potty. There is no discomfort for the child. An infant soon becomes accustomed to being regulated to about every two hours, or according to sleeping and eating intervals. Many others have also been successful in training their infants.

A HOSE WHEN HE GOES

A good friend and neighbor had a big three-year-old boy who would sit outside driving nails with a hammer and dumping in his diaper. I suggested it was time to have a man-to-man talk with the kid about the environmental implications of making such large contributions of plastic to the city dump. The father explained that he did not want to cause guilt or stifle the young man's personality. I well understood his concerns, for I have seen distraught, impatient parents doing emotional damage to their children through verbal abuse. So, I suggested a training exercise.

First, I pointed out that the boy's mother, busy with the other children, would pick up this big kid several times a day, talk sweetly to him, lay him on a bed, take off the dirty diaper, wipe him with a warm rag, rub a little lotion on the chafed spots, and then put a fresh, smooth diaper on him. Dumping in his pants was an opportunity to get his mother's undivided attention. Now, understand that there is no guilt or blame in this matter, especially on the child's part, but there is something quite inconvenient—except for the kid who loved the experience and must have found it the highlight of his day.

Next, I suggested to the father that he explain to the boy that, "Now that he was a man, he would no longer be washed in the house. He was too big and too stinky to be cleaned by the baby-wipes. From now on, he would be washed outside with a garden hose." The child was not to be blamed. Cause him to understand that this is just a progressive change in methods. At the next dump, the father took him out and merrily, and might I say, carelessly, washed him off. With the autumn chill and the cold well water, I don't remember if it took a second washing or not, but, a week later the father told me his son was now taking himself to the pot. The child weighed the alternatives and opted to change his lifestyle. Since then, several others have been the recipients of my meddling, and it usually takes no more than three, cheerful washings.

MANY SWEET RETURNS

One little, three-year-old diaper dumper, looking rather shocked when watered down with the hose. He then gritted his teeth, and adjusted to the inconvenience. When it became clear to his parents that they had a tough, resolute martyr on their hands, they continued the hosings, but sought another solution. The mother realized that since this was her last child, she just didn't want the little fellow to grow up. He enjoyed being the baby as much as she enjoyed it.

These parents, conscious of their children's nutritional needs, did not provide them with many sweets. On rare occasions when they did, it was a real treat. This little fellow was a Spartan when it came to bodily discomforts, but he sure did love the sweets. The wise mother cheerfully said to the boy, "Son, Mother has decided that you are just not old enough to be eating sweets, so until you get a little bigger and stop pottying in your clothes, you will not be allowed anything sweet." For a week he seemed to be as monkish about the sweets as he was the hose. Then the day for French toast came around. Not eating syrup, they were allowed one teaspoon of powdered sugar per toast. After watching the other children receive their powdered sugar, the forlorn fellow said to Mama, "I sure do like powdered sugar on my French toast." "I know you do," she said, "but you are not old enough yet." After his deprived breakfast of plain French toast, he climbed down, walked around to his mother, and with all the soberness of one making a revolutionary, life-time decision, he announced, "Mother, I am ready to stop wearing a diaper. Take it off." That was it. From that moment on, he took himself to the toilet. A week later, the little man, now in possession of a more disciplined character, climbed up to the table, sat down on his dry pants, and had his French toast crowned with a spoonful of powdered sugar.

A NOTE OF WARNING

Bed-wetting or diaper dumping is not a moral or character issue. It is a natural, physical function. Don't let your pride do damage to your child. No matter how ashamed or embarrassed you are, don't apply emotional pressure. He is a product of your training and conditioning.

If you have an older child who wets the bed in his sleep, under-stand, it is not a conscious act that can be corrected by the methods men-tioned above; nor is it an attitude problem that can be dealt with by dis-cipline. The problem may be physical or emotional. Regardless, buy yourself a set of plastic sheets and teach the kid to change his own bed covers. Don't ever embarrass him or cause him to feel blame.

If you suspect it could be emotional, look within yourself for the problem and get yourself adjusted. The child will grow and mature in an atmosphere of love and security.

CHAPTER 12
Child Labor

WORK DETAIL

"It's easier for me to do it," is a common reply. Another mother says, "But I feel guilty making them work, that's my job." One area in which our family was weak was the work detail. The children were given jobs here and there, but were little trained in a routine. If I was doing it over again, this area would get much more attention. In the early years, the mother is primarily responsible for this training. When a child is old enough to take a toy out of a box, he is old enough to put it back.

Mother, let your time of interaction always be training. It is natural and fun. Instead of just playing, "I'm going to get-chue," play, "Here's how we put our toys up. See, I put one up, now you put one up. That's good. You're a smart boy, and you help Mama so much." Keep the chores within the scope of their concentration. Too much will weary them; too little will prevent it from being meaningful.

When they are under five, it takes more time to be their "employer" than to be their servant. But, the best time to establish life-long habits is before five. By the time they are four or five they should feel not just wanted but needed. My Amish neighbors say that before seven the children are a drain on the family. Between seven and fourteen, they pay their way. After fourteen, they become an asset bringing in profit. By the time a child reaches seven, he should be making your life easier. A house full of seven-year-olds ought to be self-sustaining.

It is essential to a child's self-image that he feels the value of his contribution. Though he may drag in his work, he is happier when his participation is significant. Mother, if you take a little time to train when they are young, you will be able to rest when they are older.

Teach them to clean up all their own messes, and they will make fewer messes. Divide the household chores between them according to their size and ability. A child working below his ability will be bored and discontent. A child challenged will be cheerful. Don't pay or bribe a child into working. Now, an exception should be made where the work is not routine household chores. When an outside job is taken on as income, they can share in the profits in <u>realistic proportion</u> to their work.

A mother should always keep in mind that she is molding her daughters into future wives and mothers. Challenge them with sewing, cooking, cleaning, learning about everything. Let them get their hands in the dough (unless the child-training teacher is coming for dinner). From the time they are big enough to tell a tale, they should be talking about what "Mama and I did today."

Fathers, by the time the boys can follow you around, they should be "helping" you work. My boys were climbing through sawdust and stumbling over briars before they could see over the tops of my boots. They were bringing firewood in when they had to team up and roll it through the door. If you leave your sons for the women to rear, don't be surprised if at sixteen they act more like daughters.

Recently, passing a neighbor's house, we observed an interesting scene. The father was patiently standing over his two boys (one and two years old) instructing them as they folded a tarp. The little one-year-old's wobbly fat legs were held apart by a sagging diaper that obviously needed changing. But he was on his way to being Daddy's man.

When families were part of a larger family unit, or even when the boys were in public school, the absence of a father role model was less significant. Where a working father leaves his boys with a flock of girls to be homeschooled by their mother, they often lack masculinity.

Gender role distinction is demeaned in modern education. Don't let a coven of Sodomites and socialists, hiding behind the badge of professional psychologists, reprogram your natural feelings on male and female distinctiveness. <u>A boy needs a man's example if he is to grow up to be a man</u>.

WIFE, WOULD YOU SAY A WORD? (By Debi Pearl)

One of the most important aspects of child training is letting a child take on real responsibilities. Children need to see that their contribution to the running of the household is vital. Training along these lines eliminates the fighting and fussing over chores when the children get older. Spend a few minutes with each child every day, going over different chores step by step. When our younger daughter was seven years old she needed a job that required diligence, so I delegated to her the responsibility of keeping up the main bathroom. She not only kept it clean, she was responsible for seeing that it was supplied with all the necessary toiletries.

When the time came for our oldest daughter to go off to Bible College, she called her nine and eleven-year-old sisters in and passed on to them her responsibilities. As I watched her train them in the various chores, which included laundry, cooking, and kitchen clean up, I knew I had done something right. It was a change of command, a very sober and thrilling occasion for the younger girls. To the older, departing sister, it was a day of great pride to be able to entrust the younger girls with her responsibilities. Over the next year, I watched as the two younger sisters, with great dignity, assumed all her household duties.

Although I am still the mom, they are my next-in-command. I have often come home tired from a stressful counseling session to find dinner cooked, the house clean, the clothes washed, and two grinning girls doing a silly bow as I walked through the door. Many a time, after spending a long morning encouraging an overworked, overextended, exhausted mother, we would hear a cheerful call. The table would be lined with small children already eating, and a good lunch would be set for us moms. An occasion like that does more to persuade a mother than all the teaching I could ever give. For every minute you spend in training your child, you are rewarded a hundred-fold.

Our sons learned several trades before they were fourteen. They could farm, work in construction, log, hunt herbs, and cut hickory. They love working. The discipline learned in work translates into discipline in studies. No one is educated who cannot endure the routine of work. There is a certain confidence that can only be obtained through the successful labor of your hands.

Recently, there was a death among one of the Mennonite families in our community. Several of the grown brothers and sisters came back to bury their beloved brother. All of these siblings were raised with the same hard work, careful discipline, and only an eighth-grade Mennonite education. In the pine box under the apple tree, outside the old church house, lay a farmer who probably never made more than two or three thousand dollars a year.

The five brothers looking on seemed out of place in this primitive setting. One is a neurosurgeon, another is a lawyer, one a city planner, and another is a computer scientist. The fifth one has gone on to be successful in life; he is a happily married Mennonite farmer. If you consider the first four successful, know that it was not early educational opportunities that gave them the advantage. It was the confidence and ambition that comes from hard work and careful discipline in a family setting.

CHAPTER 13
Attitude Training

KEEPING LITTLE HEARTS

The attitude of your children is far more important than their actions. If their powers of concentration, faculties of discernment, and bodily disciplines were equal to their intentions, they could always be judged solely by actions. However, the infirmity of the flesh being what it is, the intentions better express the character of a child. When a child has an innocent heart, clumsiness or misjudgment can be accepted as perfection.

For instance, one mother left her little girl doing minor housework. She returned to find that the little girl had voluntarily expanded her role. She had brought in the clothes from off the line, then folded and put them away. The only problem was that some of the clothes were still damp. This mother, seeing the proud glow in her little girl's eyes, accepted the offering as perfect. It was not until after the little helper had gone out to play that the mother removed the damp clothes and returned them to the line. She later trained her little daughter to know the difference between wet and dry clothes.

Training must consider the actions, but discipline should be concerned only with the child's attitude. It is embarrassing to see a parent upset at a child for spilling milk or acting his normal, clumsy self. Judge them as God judges us—by the heart.

On the other hand, there are times when there is no disobedience, but the attitude is completely rotten. A parent must be on guard to discern attitudes. If we wait until actions become annoying to initiate discipline, we are only dealing with the surface symptoms. The root of all sin is in the heart. Know your child's heart and guard it. *"Keep thy heart with all diligence; for out of it are the issues of life (Prov. 4:23)."* It will be several years before your child can *"keep"* his own heart; until then it is entrusted to you. Let us consider some real-life examples.

SURLY TEEN

A very frazzled mother of several children, who sometimes appears as emotionally worn out as an old Confederate flag, commented on her failures with her thirteen-year-old daughter. The daughter, when asked to change a diaper on one of the small children, curled her lip in a surly manner and looked at her mother as if to say, "Why do you do this to me?" The mother received the response as added weight. After the daughter was out of hearing, the mother resignedly said, "My daughter is going to have to answer to God for herself. For awhile I felt guilty, like my sins were being reflected in my daughter; but (and her voice trailed off for lack of certainty), she will have to find God for herself."

This mother has several young children and a dread of several more on the way. With all the responsibilities of homeschooling and natural living, she is too emotionally taxed to maintain responsibility for one as old as thirteen. It was as if she was giving up on this one to pour what strength she had left into the ones coming on.

Hard work is never as draining as tension. One who is emotionally discouraged wakes up tired. The thirteen-year-old daughter, who should be a blessing and encouragement to her mother, is an added burden. If this older daughter had been given proper attitude training, the mother would not be so vexed now.

It is not impossible but much more difficult to alter the attitude of older children. They reach a point where they must be appealed to and reasoned with as one would another adult. When a child gets old enough to possess the reigns of his own heart, he must be wooed as a sinner is wooed by the Holy Spirit.

STARTING OVER

Those of you who have stair-step kids in a dismal state of disorder may be discouraged with the seeming impossibility of retraining the whole lot. Start with the young children, the ones still within an age-range to show quick improvement. Be absolutely consistent, and don't let the older ones discourage you. Their time is coming!

There is a wonderful psychological principle working for you. When the military moves into a district of general anarchy and is seen to restore order, the other districts take notice and voluntarily quiet down. Confess to your older children that you failed to properly train them—accept the blame. But now that you know better, you are going to do things differently with the younger children. The older, spoiled kids will sit back and watch. When they see the least improvement in their spoiled, little brothers and sisters they will be on your side—though they may not say so. When they become convinced of an absolutely positive transformation in the younger siblings, they will want to get on the reclamation list. As long as you remain compassionate, sane, and benevolent, they will submit to your discipline, believing it to be for their own good.

When times of anarchy do occur, your control will carry them through until their emotions settle and they can view things more objectively. When you conquer one, the others will know where you are headed and will be confident that you mean business. When you pen up a dog, he will run around searching until he is sure there is no way out, and then he will settle down. Once you convince a child that there is no alternative, he will submit.

Your children's natural self-love causes them to assume the easiest stance in any given circumstance. Your children love themselves too much to buck the inevitable. But remember, they know you as a vacillating weakling, never sticking by your principles, ignoring them when it would be inconvenient to do otherwise. They will try to make it inconvenient. Start with the youngest and work your way up. Let them know what is coming. Grin, you have secret weapons: A plan, Love, Patience, Reproof, THE ROD OF CORRECTION, and Endurance.

THROWING A FIT—TEMPER TANTRUMS

My nine- and eleven-year-old daughters came in from a neighbor's house, complaining of a young mother's failure to train her child. A seven-month-old boy, who failed to get his way, had stiffened, clenched his fists, bared his toothless gums, and called down damnation on the whole place. At a time like that, the angry expression on a baby's face can resemble that of one instigating a riot. The young mother, wanting to do the right thing, stood there in helpless consternation, apologetically shrugged her shoulders, and asked, "What can I do?" My incredulous nine-year-old answered, "Switch him." The mother responded, "I can't, he's too little." With the wisdom of a veteran who had been on the receiving end of the switch, my daughter answered, "If he is old enough to pitch a fit, he is old enough to be spanked."

PERSISTENCE

Some have asked, "But what if the child only screams louder

and gets madder?" Know that if he is accustomed to getting his unrestricted way, you can expect just such a response. He will just continue to do what he has always done to get his way. It is his purpose to intimidate you and make you feel like an overbearing tyrant. Don't be bullied. Give him more of the same. Switch him eight or ten times on his bare legs or bottom. Then, while waiting for the pain to subside, speak calm words of rebuke. If his crying turns to a true, wounded, submissive whimper, you have conquered; he has submitted his will. If his crying is still defiant, protesting, and other than a response to pain, spank him again. If this is the first time he has come up against someone tougher than he is, it may take a while. He must be convinced that you have truly altered your expectations.

There is no justification for this to be done in anger. If you are the least bit angry, wait until another time. Most parents are so guilt laden and paranoid that they are unable to carry this through to the end.

If you stop before he is voluntarily submissive, you have confirmed to him the value and effectiveness of a screaming protest. The next time, it will take twice as long to convince him of your commitment to his obedience because he has learned the ultimate triumph of endurance in this episode in which he has prevailed. Once he learns that the reward of a tantrum is a swift, forceful spanking, he will NEVER throw another fit. If you enforce the rule three times and then fail on the fourth, he will keep looking for that loop-hole until you have convinced him it will not work again.

If a parent starts at infancy, discouraging the first crying demands, the child will never develop the habit. In our home a fit was totally unknown because the first time it was tried we made it counterproductive.

PARENTAL PROTOTYPES

Never expect more of your children in the way of attitude than you are yourself. Happy, well-balanced parents that neglect the rod and reproof will have grouchy, complaining, tantrum-oriented children. But, in a situation where one or both of the parents are an emotional wreck, not much can be expected from the child. A CHILD IS GOING TO BE THE HARVEST OF HIS PARENTS' TEMPERAMENT. If the mother is sulky, critical or selfish, the children will have a tendency to be the same. If the father is a bully or full of anger and impatience, his sons will be too. If the father is rude, demanding, and disrespectful of the mother, you can expect the same from his sons. If a father is intemperate or lustful, the children will likely be worse. God says, I will visit *"the iniquities* [not guilt, and not blame] *of the fathers upon the children unto the third and fourth generation... (Exodus 20:5)."* I have seen many children despise their parents' sins, yet grow up to be just like them.

The lesson in this is: YOU MUST BE what you want your child to be—in attitude as well as actions. Don't try to "beat the ugly" out of a child that is just a display window of your own attitudes.

THEY BETTER NOT MISTREAT MY BABY

A common problem, more often found in mothers, is the "They better not mistreat my baby" syndrome. I can still remember when I was young, looking on with disgust as some swaggering brat sneered out of one side of his mouth and threatened to tell his mother. How did his parents produce such ugliness?

It's easy. Just be very protective of your child and always get emotionally involved in his disputes with other children. Let him see your anger at him being mistreated by his peers, babysitters, teachers, or other adults. Let him know you believe he is always in the right and that people are out to mistreat him, but you are there to see he gets his due. And to cap it off, when someone who is the child's senior comes to you with an accusation against your child, accuse that person of lying. When your child knows that he can control any social relationship through his threats, and that you will never believe the accusation against him, you are breeding an ugly personality.

It is not going to harm your child to be falsely accused a few times (that's life). He will have to learn to deal with it sooner or later. When he is accused, if you have doubts about his guilt, patiently search out the matter. If you determine that he has been falsely accused, tell him and then quietly drop the matter. Don't let him see your defensiveness on his behalf.

If he is roughed-up by his peers, rejoice; he is learning early about the real world. Don't make a sissy out of him. If you jump to his defense every time another child takes away a toy, pushes your child down, or even pops him in the nose, you will rear a social crybaby.

When you demand that your child be treated fairly, you are protecting him from reality. The younger they are, the easier it is for them to learn that they deserve no equality. Your reactions are not going to make life any less unfair for your child, but you can mold a feel-sorry-for-myself attitude. If you are tough he will be tough.

WHY IS EVERYBODY ALWAYS PICKING ON ME?

While I teach a Bible class, my two daughters help baby-sit a house full of children under five (five children under five is a house full). One of the mothers returned to find her three-year-old daughter whining of being mistreated by a little fellow under two. They all confirmed that the stumbling toddler had in fact provoked a class-A altercation without sufficient provocation. The older and physically superior, little girl just sat on the floor and "turned the other cheek"—only to have it walloped also. In her presence, the mother pitied the little girl and spoke critically of her assailant.

My daughters watched the situation carefully, and on several occasions observed him assaulting her. But, as the nursery workers cracked down on the mugger, he ceased his misdemeanors. (Most attacks were the result of his stumbling while practicing his walking.)

The bright and otherwise sweet little girl was very obedient, but she had developed a habit of exhibiting emotional weakness in order to get her way. She whines about everything and seems to suffer out of proportion to her happy lot in life. The young mother has cultured this tendency.

During the succeeding weeks, the mother would greet her daughter with a sympathetic inquiry as to her suffering at the hands of the twenty-four-inch nursery stalker. The nursery workers became aware that the "victim" always gave an evil report. They made it a point to watch closely, and were sure that on the occasions when there was no conflict with the alleged assailant, the little girl still gave a report of being attacked. They observed her playing happily until the mother arrived; at which time she would jump up and run into the arms of her sympathetic mother with whining tales of abuse.

As the talk escalated and the stumbling tot's infamy grew, the mother more carefully questioned her daughter. It was becoming clear that the emotionally weak girl thrived on playing the role of the abused.

One night the baby sitters observed the little girl telling the boy, "Hit me. Go on, hit me." When she finally persuaded him to reach out and strike her on the head, she would go to the workers crying of being struck. This was repeated on several occasions. Then when the protective mother arrived, the little girl had a tale of abuse to again make her the center of her mother's sympathy.

On one occasion, when the little fellow was in the other room, the girl fell down crying of being struck by him. When the mother arrived and those in charge told her that her daughter lied about being abused, she again took up for the child and denied that her daughter could lie.

I rejoice to say that this mother is one of the most teachable women I have ever met. When confronted, the mother realized she was making provision for her daughter to grow up breaking the ninth commandment: *"Thou shalt not bear false witness against thy neighbor (Exodus 20:16)."* She also realized she was cultivating a sour disposition in her little girl. She repented and immediately began working on it. The child's attitude quickly showed improvement.

BAD ATTITUDE

Bad attitude is bad through and through. For as a child *"thinketh in his heart, so is he (Prov. 23:7)." "Keep thy heart with all diligence; for out of it are the issues of life (Prov. 4:23)."* If a child shows the least displeasure in response to a command or duty, you should treat it as disobedience. If a child sticks out his lip, you should focus your training on his bad attitude. A wrong slant of the shoulders reveals a bad frame of mind. Consider this a sign to instruct, train, or discipline. A cheerful, compliant spirit is the norm. Anything else is a sign of trouble.

To those whose families have always been out of control, these goals seem ridiculous. To some who contemplate such designs on their family, this seems like an overbearing, unrealistic goal. Granted, if some families simply raised their standards to demand this level of obedience from their children, it would be overbearing. But, when approached as a revamping of the entire family, it no longer seems unreasonable. Sulking, pouting, whining, complaining, begging, and the like, should be eradicated like a bad disease.

This is not just an idealistic goal for which we generally aim, while secretly entertaining a willingness to settle for far less; it is the daily experience of many families, including our own. Like a well-cared-for garden, weeds do come up that must be dealt with, but they are never given a chance to seed. Problems do arise, but the training base we have described provides the certainty of a thriving garden of children.

CHAPTER 14
Emotional Control

THE AMISH FAMILY

When an Amish family comes over with their twelve children to visit, you would think it was a Japanese delegation, for all the self-control and order present. The children are taught to maintain control of their emotions. They are all respectful of our property and presence. When in the presence of adults, the children don't talk or play loudly. If hurt, they don't cry excessively. The children learn to give-over when another child tramples on their rights. Consistent training and discipline is the key to this kind of order.

SCREAMING TEEN

On one of those Sunday afternoons when the church was having dinner on the grounds (This is not eating off the ground. It is eating together outdoors.), a twelve-year-old girl who had been swinging on a swing set commenced to scream the cry of the imminently perishing. If one of my kids had screamed like that, I would have expected her to be caught in a people eating machine, slowly being dragged to destruction. We all threw our paper plates of food on the ground and ran to the rescue. She appeared to have fallen out of the swing, but with no perceptible damage. (We later discovered she had received one bee sting.) When the father tried to examine her for what he thought was a broken arm, she rolled and thrashed, kicked and squalled. She sounded much like someone tied to a hill of fire ants.

For the next ten minutes her father tried to get her attention, demanding to know what was wrong. She wouldn't let him examine her, but continued screaming. After ten seconds of that, I said to my wife, "She isn't hurt, she's mad."

As I returned to find my paper plate, I could occasionally hear the father's bellow over hers, "What's wrong, honey? Tell me where it hurts." I knew she wasn't hurt badly, for no one who was truly hurt could muster that much energy. Furthermore, the screaming had the sound of a protest—an assault cry.

After the men had shared a couple more fishing tales, we saw them carry her past us into the house, where her arm was eventually pronounced just fine. I was glad when they got her indoors. With the background noise, the men were starting to tell war stories. Be careful not to make emotional liars out of your children by being weak yourself.

POOR THING, WHERE DOES IT HURT?

For your children's own good, teach them to maintain control of their emotions. If you do not want to produce sissies that use adversity as a chance to get attention, then don't program them that way. When your toddler falls over on the floor, don't run and pick him up, speaking in an alarmed, sympathetic voice.

I remember, when I was only about eight years old, my cousin performed a stunt for the entertainment of all the adults present. His younger brother was sitting on the floor playing happily, when my cousin said, "Watch this." Speaking to the infant in a pitiful, compassionate voice, he said, "Oh! Is the baby hurt? Poor thing. What did you do? Does it hurt? Show it to Mama." Sure enough, my happy, little cousin puckered up, started crying, and made his way to his mother for emotional support. To the roar of the adults, she picked him up, told him it would be all right, brushed off the imaginary dirt, and sat him back on the floor to continue happily playing. I instantly programmed that away for future use. Over the years, I observed that same phenomenon many times. Only once or twice was it done deliberately for entertainment. The other times a mother was rushing to her child's real or imagined distresses. The only one enjoying it was the sympathetic mother.

TOUGH TEENS

When I was young, I determined that I would rear no sissies. When an infant fell and bumped his head, we pretended to ignore it. When a toddler took a spill, we let him lie, whimper a second, and then climb back up for another try. When a toddler fell out of the wagon or stumbled into the dirt, we let him deal with it. When the young ones wrecked their bicycles and skinned their knees, we paid no attention except to say something like, "You shouldn't go so fast until you learn to ride better." They would come in to dinner, and we would see bloody knees or skinned hands and ask, "What happened to you, Tiger?" "Oh, nothing. Just slid out on the curve in the loose gravel. I think I can make it next time." "Take it easy. Don't break something."

Now our responses, or lack of, were not unconcern; quite the contrary. There were times when we had to hold each other back in order for our child to learn the lessons of life. The times when medical attention was necessary, we administered it calmly and efficiently, returning them to their play.

Your response is important to the development of character. You do not want to produce a teenager, and ultimately an adult, who hurts himself when he needs attention.

When still a youth, I saw a teenage girl, jilted by a boyfriend, feign being hurt. I know an adult who hurts herself every time she gets emotionally disturbed. If, in your family, these extremes never occur, it is nonetheless more pleasant to live with a child or teenager who is not a "crybaby." Also, your daughter's future husband will appreciate you having trained her. And your sons will be better men.

HOLD STILL

When our first daughter was a young girl, maybe seven or eight, I looked up to see a brown-recluse spider crawling along her neck. Their bite is very cruel indeed. A pound of flesh may rot out where one bites. My daughter had been taught to trust and obey. I said, "Don't move." She froze. Not a muscle twitched. Fear paled her eyes as she followed our intense stare and felt the creature creeping up her neck. I could see the rising compulsion to slap at it, to flee screaming. She stood perfectly rigid as I slowly approached, reached out, and carefully flicked the spider away. I was thankful we had trained her to maintain control of her emotions.

THE TUMBLING TOT

I was driving my truck some distance behind a horse-drawn hay-wagon when a little fellow about four or five years old fell off the back of the wagon onto the gravel road. No one had noticed him, and the wagon continued to rattle along. I thought about going to his rescue, but he jumped up and ran to catch the wagon. After a couple of failed attempts to jump on, someone saw him and, grabbing a hand, swung him back on the wagon. After being seated, he rubbed his sore spots and continued on to the field. He did not expect the world to stop simply because he was lying in the road skinned up. I can imagine the fuss if that had happened to a modern, over-indulged, under-trained child.

CRYING BABIES, OR CRYBABIES

When 'crawlers' or 'scooters' cry, there should be a legitimate reason. If they are hungry, feed them. If they are sleepy, put them down for a nap. If they are truly hurt, allow time for the pain to subside. If they are physically uncomfortable, adjust their environment. If they are wet, change them. If they are afraid, hold them close. If they are grouchy, discipline them to get control of their self-centeredness. If they are mad, switch them. Don't let your child stay unhappy. Meet the real needs and make their selfish crying an unrewarding experience. The mother should be careful to anticipate the infant's real needs and meet them at appropriate times and levels. However, <u>when the infant is allowed to gain control of his environment through whining, he is training her</u>.

CHAPTER 15
Training in Self-Indulgence

HIS WIFE, SHE ATE NO LEAN

Early habits are lifelong habits. Why is it that some fat people find themselves compelled to eat when they become emotionally disturbed? When they get angry or depressed they go to the refrigerator as a way of coping. I have been told by grotesquely obese women that they wouldn't be fat if it were not for their compulsion to bury their disappointment under a stuffed belly.

Now, I am not attempting to define the cause of all fatness, nor even the sole cause of some; but it is at least a contributing factor in some cases. How did this connection occur? The human/animal tendency to accept conditioning is extraordinary. Every time I think of an orange and imagine eating it, I have a muscular reaction in my jaw muscles. I experience sourness when the orange is still on the tree in Florida. Through repeated experiences, I have been conditioned that way. It is involuntary. I cannot help the programmed response.

When a baby is breast-fed, there are physical limitations to how often and when he can nurse. With a bottle-fed baby—even when the bottle is given after a year of breast-feeding—the bottle becomes a mighty convenient baby-sitter. An emotionally disturbed child can be quieted by simply poking a synthetic nipple into his mouth. As the food goes in, the tension and anxiety go out. An angry child can be pacified by a "pacifier" or bottle. A child can be put to sleep with food. You can purchase for yourself a reprieve from almost anything through a bottle or pacifier. What are you doing to your child? Not only is he failing to learn self-control, <u>HE IS LEARNING TO COPE BY PUTTING SOMETHING IN HIS MOUTH</u>.

The addiction to cigarettes is not all nicotine. Have you ever noticed how a person who quits smoking will often keep something in his mouth? Many a tree has been eaten one matchstick at a time by former smokers attempting to pacify their addiction.

Many fat people have no desire for food early in the day. Not until the day's responsibilities mount up does their nervousness drive them to the refrigerator. Late at night, when the problems of the day have accumulated, the refrigerator becomes their emotional support.

I am convinced that parents who provide emotional consolation through food or the sucking sensation are training their children to be self-gratifying and indulgent. *"Temperance"* is one of the fruits of the Spirit *(Gal. 5:23)*. Parent, if you not only cater to your child's appetite, but actually employ it as a means of purchasing compliance, what are you instilling? Remember, the first human sin involved eating. The Devil's first temptation to the Son of God involved eating. *"And put a knife to thy throat, if thou be a man given to appetite (Prov. 23:2)."* There is a spiritual principle involved here that goes far deeper. To allow—much more, encourage—lack of self-control in any area is to condition the child to be generally intemperate.

INHERITED INTEMPERANCE

A parent's example of intemperance in one area may be manifested through the child by a lack of self-control in another area. Some children so despise their parents' weakness that they take special care to not fall victim. Yet, the parental example of intemperance will manifest itself in another area where their guard is not up. Parents who are intemperate in food may have skinny children that become intemperate in sex. Parents that are intemperate in possessions may have children that are intemperate in drugs. Intemperance in any area is a grave, destructive sin. Your children will reap what you sow. *"Be not deceived; God is not mocked: for whatsoever a man soweth, that shall he also reap. For he that soweth to the flesh shall of the flesh reap corruption (Gal. 6:7,8). Man shall not live by bread alone... (Matt. 4:4)."*

If, as an adult, you realize that your parents passed on their intemperance to you, you can either blame them and continue letting your belly be your god or you can throw off the curse for your sake as well as your children's.

I have sadly observed many children being trained in the art of selfish indulgence by the example of parents gathering to themselves and their children the things of this world. A child raised with commercial gadgets heaped upon his lusts is much more prone to be envious and covetous than the poor child who finds satisfaction in the simple things of life. The child who grows up deprived of nothing is greatly handicapped in real life. Never consider your affluence to be an advantage to your children. It is a handicap for which you must compensate. Examine Jesus' words regarding the disadvantages of the rich: *(Mark 4:19; Luke 12:15; 1 Tim. 6:6-19; James 5:1-5).*

CHAPTER 16
Bullies

IS EVERYONE HAVING FUN?

One of the rules—more of a principle—in our home is: "If it is not fun for all, it is not fun at all." Where there is more than one child, good, honest sparring sometimes degenerates into bullying. We kept our hands off as much as possible. If the kids were having a social conflict, we tried to let them work through it. A pecking order is inevitable, but if it got out of hand or they came to us, then we would step in to arbitrate.

BLOWING UP

Let's create a likely scenario: One of the girls is trying to blow up a balloon while the brother, several years older (who is normally very congenial with his sisters), is preventing her from accomplishing her task and laughing at her helpless protests. It starts out with her involved in the game, but she soon tires and starts to earnestly resist. He is having such fun that he continues, with increased vigor, to thwart her efforts. She is getting aggravated and complaining. He laughs louder. She starts physically resisting, jerking away, swinging her elbows, and yelling, "Stop it!" He doggedly pursues his goal of proving his prowess as chief-balloon-deflator. "OK, What's the problem?" Father asks. "Oh nothing, we're just playing," the brother says. She protests, "He won't let me blow up my balloon." So, it is time for a little training and reproof.

THE WRONG APPROACH

The wrong way to handle this would be to impatiently yell, "Give her the balloon so she will shut up and get out of here; I can't hear myself think!" He would toss it over with an "I beat you" sneer, and she would try to blow it up in his presence to prove her victory. They would continue to silently compete until another opportunity for mischief arose. This would happen between them about thirty times a day. You might switch them two or three times, to no effect. She would become a whining tattletale, and he would become a sulking bully. You are functioning like a referee who came expecting a fight, and you are there to keep it fair. You should be functioning as a teacher of righteousness.

THE RIGHT APPROACH

Try this approach. Calmly say, "What's going on here?" The brother responds, "Oh nothing, we're just playing." Daddy says, "Sister, are you having fun?" She says, "No, he won't let me blow up my balloon." Daddy says to the boy, "Are you having fun?" He looks abashed and says, "Well, we were just playing." Daddy asks, "Brother, was sister having fun?" "No, I guess not." "Could you tell that she wasn't having fun?" "Well, I guess so." "What do you mean, you guess so? Did you or did you not think she was having fun?" "Well, I knew she wasn't having fun." "Were you having fun when your sister was suffering?" Silence. "Can you have fun by making someone else unhappy?" Silence. He looks at the floor. "Look at me. How would you like it if someone bigger than you treated you like that?" "I wouldn't," he answers. Then I would say my famous lines, "If everyone is not having fun, then it is not fun. Son, you know Hitler and his men had fun when others were suffering. They laughed while boys and girls cried in pain. Do you want to grow up to be like Hitler?" In complete brokenness, he says, "No Daddy, I don't want to be like Hitler. I didn't mean to make her sad. Sister, I am sorry." What great training! The brother and sister will go away bonded and sympathetic. The sister forgives because she has seen his repentance and feels sorry for his grief. She is drawn to him. He will be more protective of her. They both have been restored.

Your reproof will produce repentance only if the boy sees genuineness in you. If he detects in you any lack of the benevolence you advocate, he will not repent. He will just become hard and bitter.

If he has taken offense at the way you have talked to Mother, he will not experience repentance until you express the same. If the boy does not show repentance after it is clear he understands the issues, a spanking would be in order, then further reproof and reasoning. If there is still no repentance issuing in forgiveness and love to his sister, then it becomes clear he has a deeper, more long-term problem, one that requires rebuilding of relationships.

CHAPTER 17
Religious Whips

HATERS OF GOD

I have cringed at seeing parents use God to intimidate their children into obedience. A child has been "bad," and the mother warns, "You shouldn't do that, God doesn't like it." Or, "God is going to get you for that." Again, "Mama might not see it but God does." Talking about negative, counter-productive training! If you constrain a child by threatening him with divine displeasure, he will come to hate God and will throw off religion as soon as he is old enough for independent action. It happens with regularity. Never, I say, "<u>NEVER use God to threaten or intimidate your child into compliance.</u>" You are causing the child to associate God with condemnation and rejection.

When I was a young teenager at summer camp, there were several boys who got rowdy late at night. The angry directors disciplined them by making them sit and read the Bible. About 2 AM, I got up to *"ease myself abroad (Deut. 23:13)"* and saw them sitting there with open Bibles in their laps, wearing surly expressions. At that young age, yet loving the Scripture myself, and while knowing nothing of psychology, I distinctly was grieved for what I knew was going to be the results of this "discipline." The staff was conditioning these young men to hate the Bible. With a burning resentment in their hearts, every time they looked down at its pages they were associating the Bible with a bitter spirit. Three or four hours of this could leave an aversion for Scripture that, with further reinforcement, could continue throughout the rest of their lives.

I know a mother who makes her children look up Bible verses for punishment. The exercise itself could be good training—except when it occurs as a way of dealing with rebellion. The rebellion should be resolved by the rod and correction.

GOOD MEMORIES ARE WELCOMED

Don't use your devotional time as a clearinghouse for settling grievances. Family worship should never be a time to "call someone on the carpet." No one has good feelings about being called to the principal's office. The school principal did the really serious paddling when I was in school. I have lived nearly a half-century and still feel apprehension when going into the office at a public school. He and I had a couple of serious encounters. One of these days I am going to make an effigy of a school principal and then tell him to bend over and grab his ankles.

On the other hand, when I see pastel chalk, I remember old Mrs. Johnson, my art teacher, smiling and setting up a still-life for us to draw. I would go back there and spend hours, if I could.

What memories and associations are you filing away in your child's subconscious? Teach the Bible in your home. Give them exercises of looking up verses on patience, love, faithfulness, and so forth, but don't do it as a response to their failure in some area. If they should have a weakness which needs instruction, wait until the pressure and condemnation is off before giving them a study that involves their weakness. If there are guilt feelings present, the lesson will only bring further condemnation and isolation that the rod cannot absolve. When the instruction about God is separate from your discipline, they are free to make an association without feeling watched and graded. Otherwise, you will end up with children working for God's approval, as well as yours. Allow the Spirit of God to apply truths to your child's consciousness. An adult's sense of discernment is more highly developed. Don't cause them to have a foreboding of God before they are mature enough to see everything in perspective.

CHAPTER 18
Imitations

CHRISTIAN PARENTS' PARROTS

One way to dull your children's sensitivity to God is to make them religious showoffs. Parents who value the outward displays of devotion often fall into the Pharisee syndrome. Don't train your children in the skills of pretense. Don't train them to be *"as the hypocrites are: for they love to pray standing in the synagogues and in the corners of the streets, that they may be seen of men. Verily I say unto you, they have their reward (Matt. 6:5)."*

The other day, I invited my family out to see our dog do a new trick. I gave the command, but he was too distracted by them to regard me. I had interrupted their schedule with the promise of a trick, and the dog acted as if he had never seen me before, much less knew what I was saying. I became anxious and started pushing him to perform. He was making me look silly. "What right does he have to do this to me? Me, of all people. My family would have thought I was so smart, and now I look dumb. Stupid dog. Must be inbred." Sensing my disapproval, he started to shy away from me. To get my approval, he must make me look good in public. After all, what is a dog good for, but to elevate his master?

I have had parents bring their little child in, stand him in front of me, and say, "Say 'praise the Lord' for Brother Mike." When he has finished his performance, everyone smiles and praises him. The parents grin as if they just heard the announcement that their dog had won the annual Frisbee catching contest. When little children are cute in their prayers or religious imitations they should be totally ignored. Otherwise you encourage hypocrisy. Never give them a *"form of godliness."* It is a cheap trick to school your children to appear ahead of their peers in religious devotions. You and your children are rewarded here and now; and that is all the reward such stage playing ever gets. *"Verily I say unto you, they have their reward (Matt. 6:5)."*

One well-meaning father has two children who sing fairly well. Every chance he gets, he captivates an audience to listen to their singing. Their gospel songs, sung by another, would be a blessing; but when sung in exhibition as a way of showing off, it is a pain to endure. Their singing is so cute. As they parade back to their seats, he praises them, smiling like I would have been if my dog had only performed for me.

One time when the two singing "parrots" forgot the words and showed a little indifference to performing, the audience became restless, and the father became anxious. His act was falling apart. He coaxed and encouraged until I saw in him the same feelings I had toward my non-performing dog. Now the dog is not going to suffer from being paraded, but these children already are suffering. The father's ambition for himself and his children overrides his concern for their spiritual well-being. Or, maybe he doesn't have the wisdom to discern the difference. It is easy to come to ruin in this satanically controlled world.

CHAPTER 19
Homeschool Makes No Fools

THE SYSTEM

One judge in Nebraska said that the public educational system is preparing the children of America for merger into the New World Order. He went on to say that the children of Christian homeschool families would not fit into their planned system.

Never even consider sending your children to private Christian schools, much less the public, automaton factories. Whether a classroom is based completely on Christian education or secular principles is not the issue (although, we would by far prefer Christian). God didn't make teenage boys and girls to sit together in a classroom every day while real life outside passes them by. The world's system digs a pit and then creates a myriad of industries to reclaim the tragic lives that fall into it. Classroom education for the young is a pit. The psychiatrists, counselors, social workers, Planned Parenthood, policemen, social manipulators, juvenile courts, drug dealers, penal institutions, pharmaceutical companies, and medical doctors stand on the edge of the pit competing for the business generated by the shovels of the National Education Association.

One warning: There exists a fundamental fault that is demonstrated in the discouragement experienced by many homeschool families. The public educational system is based on false premises. Therefore, both its curriculum and its format are in error. The homeschool is not established to duplicate the public school in a private environment, yet most homeschoolers are attempting to do that very thing. The stress on the family attempting to perform for the sake of public image, as well as state required testing, is destructive to the emotional and intellectual development of the child.

Ask yourself the question, "If I did not have to answer to anyone, and I were not controlled by public opinion, what would I desire for my children to learn in their early years?" Keep in mind that specialty disciplines necessary for professional employment need not be taught by either the classroom or the homeschool. Those things can be learned when the child is emotionally mature and ready to enter the workplace.

Parents, you are wearing yourself out trying to keep up with the judges. Teach from your heart, not from the John Dewey perspective. <u>Children need a mother who teaches them, not a teacher who doesn't have the emotional energy to mother them. Young men need a father who teaches them to work, not a father too busy working to teach them.</u>

The best schooling for children is a good home life, not a home that is all school. It is a strange perversion to remove a child from that which is natural to life and make of him a professional student. Don't accept the false premise that academic and behavioral education is the foundation of life and society. Order your own life according to God's perspective. Your children are too valuable for you to compromise.

After homeschooling for over sixteen years, we have seen the fruit of our "philosophy" of child rearing. Our oldest just finished her first year in college with a 4.0 grade point average.

If you fear your children are too isolated from the world and need what the socialists call "socialization," then get yourself a TV and sit them down in front of Hollywood for about two hours every day. They will soon be duplicates of the public school, local hang out, back-alley morality. Put your children to the breast of Hollywood and they will never be nurtured on the *"milk of the word."* Hollywood is a far more effective teacher than you will ever be, and it has an aggressive, appealing agenda.

If you want a child who will integrate into the New World Order and wait his turn in line for condoms, a government funded abortion, sexually transmitted disease treatment, psychological evaluation, and a mark on the forehead, then follow the popular guidelines in education, entertainment, and discipline. But if you want a son or daughter of God, you will have to do it God's way.

I am forty-eight years old. [fifty-five years old at the time of this revised edition] My oldest son is seventeen, and my youngest is fifteen. [They now range from seventeen to twenty six.] There is always the possibility that I could be gone by the time they have children of their own. When I think about them getting married and rearing children, there is so much I would like to see them keep in mind. So, in summary, I will address a letter to my two sons.

CHAPTER 20
Personal

LETTER TO MY SONS
Gabriel and Nathan Pearl,

I cannot imagine the kind of world tomorrow will bring, but unless it is the Millennium spoken of in the Bible it will be even more hostile to the family. If the Lord should tarry long enough for you to marry and begin rearing children, your dad has a few words of advice.

First, know that the woman you marry will be the lifelong mother of your children. All that she is in the accumulation of past experiences will be present as the mother of your children. There is not a more major decision affecting the future of your children than the choice of your life's partner. The relationship between a man and his wife has more effect on the children than any other factor. A couple may express their differences only in private, but they cannot hide the effects from their children. Remember, your family will be no better than the relationship you have with your wife—their mother.

Be sure to cultivate your relationship with your wife. Meet her needs. Make her happy. Her state of mind is going to be 50% of your children's example, 100% when you are not there. If you will love and cherish your wife, the children will love and cherish her also. If you are a servant to her, the example will translate to their experience.

When you look for a wife and mother for your children, the first qualification is that she <u>love the Lord</u> and be His disciple. Nothing else will keep her for the duration. She will need to know how to pray. A girl who takes Christ for granted will do the same with her family. A man and his wife are *"heirs together of the grace of life (1Pet. 3:7)."* It takes two, equally yoked, to pull the family wagon safely through the hostile deserts of this life.

The second thing to look for in a prospective wife is <u>cheerful-ness</u>. Now, some might ignore this qualification altogether; but I can't emphasize too forcefully the value and practicality of this quality. A girl who is unhappy and discontent before marriage will NOT suddenly change afterwards. Everyone has trials and adversities. The happy, cheerful girl has learned to deal with them and still enjoy life. No man can make a discontented woman happy. A woman who does not find joy from a wellspring within will not find it in the difficulties and trials of marriage and motherhood.

Courtship is a garden in spring—everybody's looks promising; but marriage is a garden in August, when the quality of the soil and seed and the care to guard against pestilence, blight, and weeds begins to manifest itself. The fruit of the womb can be spoiled before germination. Give prayerful care to the choice of a wife and mother. A girl who gets her feelings hurt and cries in order to manipulate you will be a ball and chain after you are married. Cheerfulness shows up best when things are not exactly the way she likes them.

The next quality to look for is <u>thankfulness</u>. When a young girl is unthankful toward her family or her circumstances, a change of environment and relationships is not going to make her thankful. Thankfulness is not a response to one's environment, rather, an expression of the heart. Avoid a moody, unthankful, unhappy girl. If she is not full of the joy of living before marriage, she surely will not be afterwards. A young lady who had been married less than a month said to Deb, "I have never in my life been one to have my feelings hurt. But, since I got married, I seem to go around with a chip on my shoulder. I guess it is just that I care more than I once did." Deb told her, "No, you don't care more; you just feel that you have more rights, and therefore expect more." The thing to remember is that personalities and temperaments do not improve after marriage. When the social restraints are lifted, the freedom that comes from a secure union permits one to express true feelings.

Boys, take note of a girl's attitude toward her father. It doesn't matter what kind of louse he may be, if she is rebellious to him, she will be twice as rebellious to you. If she speaks disrespectfully of or to her father, she will do likewise toward you.

Another thing to look for is a <u>creative hard worker</u>. Don't marry a lazy, slothful girl. Beauty can get mighty old lying up in bed framed in a disheveled, griping, slothful pout. Whatever you do, avoid a lazy girl. If she expects to be waited on, let her marry a waiter. You will have a full job rearing the children without having to rear a wife.

Never marry a girl who feels she is not getting the best man in the world when she gets you. A girl who enters marriage thinking she could have done better will never be satisfied for wondering what it might have been like if....

Avoid the girl who is enamored with her own looks. Better to marry a homely girl who is content to love and be loved than one who is going to spend her years trying to maintain her fading beauty. Life is too big and full to be spent waiting on a disappointed woman who is regretfully looking in the mirror.

Avoid like the plague the girl who would pursue her own career outside the home. A wife must be your "help-meet."

The last qualification is a <u>love for children</u>. A girl who doesn't want her life encumbered with children is suffering a deep hurt and is walking a road to misery. One day, the Lord willing, you are going to have children of your own.

Now, I want to speak to you about being good fathers. While you are still young and unmarried, with no children, do what all of God's creatures do—prepare the nest for their arrival. DON'T PUT YOURSELF IN AN OCCUPATIONAL POSITION THAT WILL LEAVE YOU OUT OF POSITION TO BE A GOOD FATHER. Plan your life's trade so as to maximize your role as father. Fathers who become absorbed in their success in business will make lousy fathers. If you gain the whole world and lose your child's soul, what profit is it? Some workaholics will say they are doing it for their children—providing security, a good education, etc. Why is it that the children of hard working, absent fathers never appreciate their sacrifice, and even show disdain and contempt for their father's success? The reason is that children are not fooled. They understand their father's absence to be lack of interest. They believe his career to be selfishly motivated. They see their father getting more satisfaction from his job than from their presence. Whether this be true or not, the results are the same. Business success always passes away; your children are eternal. The education your child will need cannot be purchased at a university. It is purchased by the father in the many hours spent doing things with his children.

The concept of "quality" time as opposed to "quantity" is a salve for the consciences of modern parents wrapped up in worldly pursuits. A scheduled hour of clinical-like attention makes your "quality time" nothing more than the fulfillment of a business appointment—a therapy session. It can be unreal and pretentious. Insincere attention to inconsequential matters cheapens fellowship. Your best time together will be that which is spent in real struggles to achieve common goals. A child will build self-worth, not by being the center of attention in idle chatter, but by actually conquering a real world need—putting up a mail box, a clothes line, cutting the grass, bringing in firewood, washing windows, building a dog house, going on the father's job and being a real helper.

Do you remember when Don Madill would come to work in our cabinet shop with his little two- or three-year-old son hanging around, cleaning up sawdust or hammering a nail? There was no pretense or haste in that father-son relationship. Today, his sons are little men, secure in their role.

As soon as your first child is born, begin your role as father. Relieve your tired wife for a couple of hours by taking the infant and attending to all his needs. When you are reading or resting, lay the child on your lap. When you boys were only a few days old I would lay you on my chest to sleep out a restless night. I got to where I could sleep soundly with your little puddle on my chest. Your exhausted mother needed a little break.

When I was newly married, I expected my wife to be a super woman. I soon learned that if she was going to last through several more child-births, and that in good spirits, she was going to need a lot of support. Treat your wife as a delicate flower, and she will have the energy to be a more giving mother.

I am aware that you boys don't need much sleep. However, if you experienced a major operation every two to three years, having a twenty-pound tumor removed, and you had to lend your body to a dairy farmer, you would need more rest also. Allow your wife to sleep a little longer than you do, and she will be more efficient.

Though I spent a lot of time with you when you were young, I always told your mother, "They are yours until they can follow me outside, and then they are mine." Take your little ones along on many adventures. Explore and discover the world all over again with each one. I would take you rabbit hunting in a backpack. My rabbit dogs got so conditioned that when they saw a backpack they thought we were hunting. I think Rebekah was glad when Gabriel came along and displaced her from the rumble seat.

Provide lots of junk for your children to exercise their creativity—cardboard boxes, wooden blocks, sawdust, sand, sticks, hammers, and nails. Avoid store-bought playthings that can stifle creativity by limiting imagination.

An important principle to remember is that the more time you spend doing things together, the fewer discipline problems you will have. A child who adores his father will want to please him in everything. A child can't rebel against his best buddy. When they are big enough to look at pictures in a book, spend time turning pages with them. When they are old enough to understand, begin reading or telling Bible stories. Throughout the day, as it is natural, tell them of our heavenly Father. Together, examine nature as the wise creation of a magnificent God.

Don't put off spending time being a daddy. Each day they grow without you is like a tomato plant growing without being staked. It spreads without direction. The weeds come up inside where they cannot be removed. The fruit will be brought forth on the ground where it will rot.

A father who is "there," always involved in his child's life, will know the heartbeat of his child. If you will praise and reward the desired behavior, there will be very little undesirable behavior. You will be speaking fifty encouraging words for every rebuke.

But, don't fall prey to the modern psychological substitute of neglecting a child and then running in to say something positive. It is artificial, and it is flattery. Positive statements that are not warranted by legitimate works are destructive. A child should know that he has earned every praise. Praise not based on deserving works is as unjust as is punishment without provocation. It will teach a lie, in that it reverses reality. There is no substitute for real-life presence. If your child is not doing anything praiseworthy, then take his hand to walk beside you until he does do something worthy. Neglected children become rejected children. A child must have his father as a plant must have light to grow healthy. A flash bulb approach is not sufficient. A slow, steady shining of the father's presence is what is needed.

Don't ever leave the spiritual training to their mother (no matter how good a job she does). Otherwise, the children will grow up thinking religion is for women. You put the children to bed in the evening, and read and pray with them.

As your boys get older, make sure they are not confined to studies too much. By the time they are twelve or thirteen, they should be finished with structured school and be involved in an occupation with you. Continue to expose them to concepts and ideas; but, above all, provide real life problems that they must solve—bicycle, small engine, or appliance repair. All forms of building and maintenance are essential training.

The concept you are seeking to convey is one of independence and confidence. A child who can do it, fix it, make it, will try new things and expect to succeed. The confidence in work will translate to success in education.

Remember the twenty-seven-year-old Amish fellow, with his first car, going off to college in a far away city, leaving all the things that were familiar, facing challenges never before considered. I was apprehensive about his ability to succeed in this new environment. He had none of the necessary skills. His educational ability was about equal to that of a sixth-grader.

When I tried to warn him of the difficulties ahead, he said, "I have always been able to do everything I tried to do, I can do this also." It was hard on him, but he got a "B" average the first semester. Whether it was the product of his hands or his head, he had learned to succeed.

If you burden a young child with studies to the point of making him feel inadequate, you are building a principle of failure into him. First, teach your children to work with their hands, and the education of their minds will come more readily. Don't leave your boys at home with mother and the girls in a classroom setting. They should be out with the men.

Boys, guide your wives to understand training and discipline. Don't take for granted that they are automatically prepared to be mothers. Some mothers don't have the courage to discipline. They will tell the children, "Just wait until your daddy gets home, he will spank you." When you walk through the door, you will want the kids to all come climbing on your legs and pulling on your arms, not cowering in a corner. Three hours of dreading Daddy's coming home can be devastating programming. Cause your wife to do her own discipline.

Check yourself for balance by asking the question, "Do my children view me as a stern and severe disciplinarian or as a cheerful and wonderful companion and guide?" <u>Your judgments and punishments should be lost in the many hours of happy communion.</u>

Lastly, as your children develop, let them feel a part of the struggles of life. Don't become so "successful" that you can provide everything they need or want. If you find that everything is coming too easily, give it all away and start over under more difficult circumstances.

Life without struggle has no achievement. If they lose their shoes, let them go without until they can make the money to buy more.

Make sure you do not have all the delicacies available to eat. Let them learn to be content doing without.

Keep the sugar and junk food out of the house. If they never have it, they will not want it. If eating between meals prevents them from eating real food (meat, potatoes, vegetables, salads, etc.), then don't let them eat except at mealtime.

There are some flavors or textures that we just have an aversion for. Allow each child one or two dislikes; just don't let their preferences be too limited. If a child doesn't like what is on the table, let him do without until the next meal. A little fasting is good training. If you get a child who is particularly finicky and only eats a limited diet, then feed him mainly what he doesn't like until he likes it.

Forget about buying them toys. Some functional toys are desirable, like a metal truck for the little boys, or a tricycle or bicycle for the older ones. Little girls can profit from play dishes and baby dolls (which resemble real babies). Just don't cultivate their covetous inclinations by teaching them to expect to have their lusts indulged.

Never yield to the fads. Christians should have too much dignity to be carried along by the Madison Avenue promoters. Their shoes, clothes, and cereals should be chosen for serviceability, not style.

Hollywood is not for God's children. Don't allow the brainless, subversive, Sesame Street type propaganda to come into your house. Your children's thinking should be molded by the Word of God and Christian example, not by sex perverts and socialists. If you want to destroy your family then get yourself a good TV and VCR to keep the kids company.

The Christian family is a mother and father with children, all living, laughing, loving, working, playing, struggling, and achieving together for the glory of God.

You must have a vision bigger than the here and now. You are not preparing your child for time, but for eternity. Adam begat a son in his own likeness. You will beget sons and daughters in your image. All earthly endeavors should anticipate eternity. As your child bears the image of his earthly parents, he must be caused to bear the image of his Heavenly Father. Born in your image, he must be born-again into Christ's image. To be conformed to the image of God's Son is our expectation and hope. It is a colossal ambition, but we have the resources of heaven at our disposal.

Wisdom is given upon request. Love is the only commandment; self is our greatest enemy; the Bible is our only educational resource; the Holy Spirit is our comforter; the blood of Christ is our only hope. Let us run the race that is set before us *"for as much as you know that your labor in the Lord is not in vain (1Cor. 15:58)."*

LETTER FROM MOM TO THE GIRLS (by Debi Pearl)
Rebekah, Shalom, and Shoshanna Pearl,

Life is full of choices. There are choices you will make while you are still young that will help fashion your life as well as that of your children. Helping you prepare to make wise decisions has been our goal.

God said of Abraham, *"For I know him, that he will command his children and his household after him, and they shall keep the way of the LORD, to do justice and judgment; that the LORD may bring upon Abraham that which he hath spoken of him (Gen. 18:19)."* Preachers have often pondered why God chose Abraham to be the father of the Jewish nation. God knew Abraham would *"command his children"* (teach them to walk uprightly).

When the time comes for you to consider marriage, think about this: can this young man be trusted with God's heritage? It is not only your life he will touch, but the lives of your children and your children's children. Abraham's teaching was so effective that his son Isaac was willing to trust his father and submit to the sacrificial knife. Again, Isaac had confidence in his father's judgment when Abraham sent a servant to his kindred to choose a wife for him. Abraham knew it would take a chosen woman for the chosen man to continue the lineage.

Remember to be a helper to your husband. Stand behind your man with prayer, encouragement, and trust. Honor him, bless him, and serve him as unto the Lord. He will thrive before God in this environment. As he grows, your children will grow, and your cup will be so full it will overflow into the lives of others.

When you are peeved with him for some silly offense, remember you are cutting off the prayer line. Don't allow hurt feelings to fester and disease the relationship. Be cheerful, thankful, and ready to forgive. Your children will watch you. If you show disregard, disapproval, anger, irritation, or dishonor to your husband, it will open the door for the children to do the same—not only to their father, but, in a greater degree, to you. In Proverbs it speaks of this very thing: *"Every wise woman buildeth her house: but the foolish plucketh it down with her hands (Prov. 14:1)."*

Begin training your children early; don't wait until there is a problem. A one-year-old baby who hesitates before obeying is developing a habit that will bring grief as he gets older. What your child is at two, he will be at twelve, only magnified many times over. *"Even a child is known by his doings, whether his work be pure, and whether it be right (Prov. 20:11)."* Don't expect your child to suddenly grow into a God-fearing adult. Adults spend their lives living out their formative years. Adults are just old children.

Don't let the cares of the family, the church, and the world steal the time needed to maintain holy matrimony. The time spent being a good wife is the deep root that nourishes the whole plant. Have a sanctuary where no child is allowed. There are times when being a good mother means teaching the children that, "This is OUR time, and you had better find something to occupy you elsewhere."

CONCLUDING THOUGHTS BY DEBI PEARL

All that you have read is what we have put into practice in rearing our children. You can rear happy, obedient, temperate, even God-fearing children that are still lost and undone before God. There is more to knowing God than techniques and principles. There has to be that living, breathing life that only the Holy Spirit of God can give.

Do not get caught up in pouring your life into a good cause—even the rearing of a large family. Pour your life into knowing and serving the Savior and seeking that every life you touch be touched with the knowledge of forgiveness in the shed blood of Jesus.

We are called to be soldiers in the army of the living God. Raising up young, new recruits is exciting. Children that see God in action, saving souls and changing lives, are seeing something real, something eternal.

When one of our daughters came back from a missionary trip to Central America, I asked her about the missionaries' children. Her reply startled me. "The missionaries' kids have a vision to be the one to reach the next tribe. They are aware of the lost and dying tribe with no one to go unless they fill the gap. They spend their youth preparing and planning for that tribe. They know what they want to be when they grow up. They want to be the one who breaks the language and tells that tribe the story of Christ. They grow up with purpose, the purpose that those who have never heard might hear."

CHAPTER 21
Conclusion

(By Michael Pearl)

I have had many parents look despondent and say, "I have waited too long. My children are too old to train." It is true that the older children get the harder it is to mold them. Yet, no human being ever gets too old to have his actions conditioned—as military boot camps demonstrate. But only in a controlled environment, where the threat of force is real, can a rebel be brought to bay. When a child gets old enough to seriously contemplate leaving, the power-discipline will lose its effectiveness. You may not be able to recover everything with a fourteen-year-old, but you can see such improvement as to make it seem a miracle. The ten-year-old is still quite moldable. The earlier you start, the better, but as long as they live, it is never too late.

It is likely one parent is going to read this book and revamp the training and discipline, while the other may be content to continue with the status quo. Mother, if you decide to stop giving the children "chances," while your husband continues to play the threatening game, you will be tempted to have critical feelings. That will be your pride manifesting itself. Your bitterness at your husband and the division that the children detect will make matters worse. Your husband's pride will cause him to be even more resistant, lest he be the disciple of his critical wife and some unknown author.

Mother, make your husband envious. While your husband is away, be so consistent and thorough that you gain perfect, instant obedience from your children. Do not strive with your husband. Don't demand cooperation. Train them while he is gone. Spank them when he is away. They will learn that no matter how careless Daddy is, Mama is the "law of God Himself." Once you are in charge, when you see him failing to gain obedience, at an appropriate time, in his presence, quietly command the children, and they will run to obedience. After several days of this, he will ask, "How do you do it; they don't obey me that way?" Just humbly smile as you hold up the switch and say, *"The rod and reproof give wisdom (Prov. 29:15)."* Then demurely turn and walk away. He will become jealous.

If you are not critical—and only if you are not critical—will he want to know more of your secret. The change in your attitude towards the children (no more anger, no arguments, quiet control) will get your husband's attention. However, if the only change he sees is that you are spanking the children more, and in equal proportions you are angry with him, he will think that it is just a hormonal imbalance that will hopefully run its course.

FINALLY

Reading back over the text, it seems that I have given a lot of negatives—what not to do, and what is wrong. If I were simply giving instruction for laying out a flower garden, it could all be quite positive; but if a surgeon is instructing student doctors on heart surgery, there will be a lot of negatives. A procedure so invasive requires cautious, narrow limitations with needful warnings. That which is successfully accomplished every day can end in tragedy if done negligently. Child rearing is an invasive procedure. You invade the soul of a developing human being, an eternal living soul. It is not an inconsequential procedure. The whole heavens stand in the waiting room in anticipation of the outcome.

If after reading this you feel frustrated and discouraged, don't attempt to implement these techniques. This is not something that can be TRIED or applied a little at a time. It takes insight and confidence to endure. If this is all new to you, and you have some doubts, you will not make it through the trials. You should read it again and follow it up with our books, No Greater Joy Volume One, Volume Two and Volume Three.

On the other hand, if I have put into words the things you have known all along but never been able to articulate, and these concepts are in your heart, and you are totally convinced of the right of what we have said, then by God's grace you will see results.

Let me close with the words of a four-year-old. A family who had been applying these truths for only a week was visiting us in our front yard. Preparing to leave, the father called their new dog. The excited dog teased the man by running off just as he got within reach. The father became irritable and started speaking critically of the dog's intelligence. Pleading on behalf of the dog, the four-year-old son said, "But Daddy, you haven't trained him yet!"

Free Magazine

In response to the many questions we receive, we publish a bi-monthly magazine–**No Greater Joy**. It addresses the ongoing issues of child training, marriage, and family. You can become a subscriber by simply sending us your name and address.

Once on our mailing list, you will also receive notification of any seminars taught by the Pearls in your area.

Write today and receive a free subscription to our magazine.

No Greater Joy Ministries, Inc.
1000 Pearl Road
Pleasantville, TN 37147
United States of America

www.NoGreaterJoy.org

Other books
by *Michael Pearl*

To Train Up a Child
No Greater Joy Volume One
No Greater Joy Volume Two
No Greater Joy Volume Three
Romans–Commentary
By Divine Design
Repentance
To Betroth or Not to Betroth
Pornography–Road to Hell
In Defense of *Biblical* Chastisement
Holy Sex

No Greater Joy Ministries, Inc.
1000 Pearl Road
Pleasantville, TN 37147
United States of America
www.NoGreaterJoy.org